D0044460

OTHER BOOKS BY STEPHEN J. BODIO

On the Edge of the Wild

Querencia

Aloft

Rage for Falcons

Eagle Dreams

SEARCHING FOR LEGENDS IN WILD MONGOLIA

STEPHEN J. BODIO

The Lyons Press

Guilford, Connecticut
An imprint of The Globe Pequot Press

The Lyons Press is an imprint of The Globe Pequot Press.

10 9 8 7 6 5 4 3 2 1

Printed in the United States of America

Designed by Leanna Weller Smith

Map by Stefanie Ward

ISBN 1-59228-207-5

Library of Congress Cataloging-in-Publication Data is available on file.

To Canat Cheryiasdaa, guide, soldier, ever-cheerful
companion, friend;
and for Libby, who once again made it easy

"Life has not stopped and the world is not really a museum, yet."

Ted Hughes

"The beginnings of my own journey did not lie in scientific study, nor was I sent on a "mission" or "expedition" of any kind. I came to it more in the way of an old man dreaming a dream or a young man seeing a vision."

Owen Lattimore, *The Desert Road to Turkestan*

AUTHOR'S NOTE

Recently I read an item in *Atlantic Monthly* where it was alleged that those who went on difficult trips and wrote about them were now called "explornographers"—derivation self-evident. *Honni soit qui mal y pense,* but I hope this book offers a bit more than titillation.

My "flying visit" begins in libraries and photographs, rambles around in memories, goes to Brooklyn and Wyoming, to New Mexico, and to the New England of my youth before it ever leaves the States for an exotic place. It is a little bit about moving around in time, but, though it contains facts about faraway places and strange animals, it is not just about moving through space. If you want straight narrative, I'd suggest you skip forward to Part II.

On orthography: there is none, yet. My friend Canat, who speaks five languages, spells his wife's name two ways and the name of the town where he lives in three. Our friend spells his name "Aralbai," but another book spells it "Orolobai." A biologist of my acquaintance spells his name Munkhtsog, but still another book spells it "Montsukh." I even know a businesswoman who spells her own name two ways. And that's without getting into historical (i.e. nineteenth century) spellings. Mongolia has several languages, and has had three scripts. I merely attempt to split the difference.

In order to make the narrative more comprehensible and less repetitive, I have altered and shortened the time line and the order of the "in-country" section a bit. Nothing significant has been omitted.

—Stephen J. Bodio

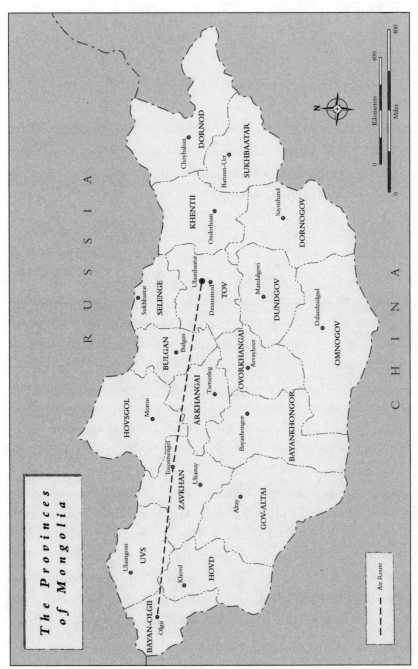

The Provinces of Mongolia

Prologue

In morning light, the riders make three black sil-louhettes above a blacker crest of volcanic rock. Their fur hats, crested with feathery plumes, are not of our time. At each horseman's right side sits another figure, not human, head as high as the rider's, giving them an oddly unbalanced look.

Widen the focus and the country instantly reduces the humans and their companions to insignificance. To the east, our right, the ridge rises in sharp steps into walls and blocks and masses of white until it is lost in clouds of snow, though the sun shines brilliantly in a pale sky. The ridge falls steeply away from the riders' feet to where we stand on a stony plain, golden in the low-angled sunlight, lightly frosted with snow in the hollows where the wind hasn't blown it away. To our left, the ridge juts into a broad pass, braided for two miles with tracks and ruts leading north to the little city of Bayaan Olgii thirty miles away, south into the Altai mountain range. Across the pass rise hills, ridges, finally more mountains on the far western horizon. There isn't a tree, green twig, nor human habitation in sight.

Beyond the western mountains are Siberia, Kazakhstan, China. Behind us is a boxy green Russian van standing high on a four-wheeler chassis. I raise my binoculars to the riders above us and they blur, then snap into focus. I am perched at nine thousand feet, and the air is still and absolutely clear.

The first rider, the oldest, is Manai, whom I have known for three years: a Kazakh, a Mongolian citizen, a master of eagles. He is fifty, a year younger than I am, but his long face with its high cheekbones is etched by the long winters and desert climate of his home. Winds and exposure and forty-below temperatures, endured on horseback and motorcycles, have chipped and loosened his teeth; he is missing an incisor. But his green eyes, as piercing as his eagle's, have never needed glasses to see their quarry.

I had hoped to ride the ridge this morning, but if I did, Kadan, Manai's oldest son, would have had to lend me his horse. Instead we—my guide and friend Canat, who is also Manai's cousin, my wife Libby, and I—decided to drive over a saddle in the ridge. I would get out and scramble along below the horsemen to block any quarry's escape downhill, while Canat and Libby continued to the plain below, from which they would attempt to photograph the action.

I am fairly fit and live at 6,500 feet when I'm home in the mountains of New Mexico. Still, after a few minutes, I am panting in the chilly air. Although it is October, the temperature is about fifteen degrees F in the shade, and only a bit warmer in the sun. The horses are moving slowly, though, and I manage to keep parallel to them.

Manai has unhooded his eagle so that her eyes, even better than his, can search for prey. Yesterday she had missed a shot at a wolf on this same ridge; now, frustration has made her even more eager. She rides erect and bristling, turning her head from side to side. Manai had told us that the boulders of the mountain hid many foxes, and that, sooner or later, a flush was inevitable. I hoped so. I had been waiting a long time for this.

Time ticks away. The only sounds are the click of the horses' hooves, the creak of their saddles, an occasional low word from Manai, and the sound of my breathing. Then, with no warning at all, the eagle is off the glove, stroking, climbing forward.

I cannot see the fox at first. The eagle hits the wind as she tops the ridge but, instead of falling back, she cuts into it and rises like a kite. Manai gallops forward at a speed that seems reckless on the loose rocks, shouting. Now the fox appears, fawn-colored and supple, cascading down the rocky steps like a furry waterfall. The eagle towers two hundred feet above, turns, and falls like a hammer. The fox dodges once, but somehow the eagle is now ahead of him, turning. The two arcs of movement converge in a cloud of dust, and all is still.

I AM A FALCONER, AMONG OTHER THINGS, AND MY LOVE FOR birds has brought me to many strange places and shown me many strange sights. This was not my first flight, nor my second, nor my two hundredth. I have hunted grouse with gyrfalcons on the high plains, and rabbits in industrial junkyards in the eastern cities, hawked on snowshoes in Maine and in sweltering heat in the Sonoran desert. I once nearly drowned in a salt marsh creek on Cape Cod, trying to retrieve a duck my bird had knocked down. I have corresponded about falconry with an Afghan prince, and had an eighty-seven-year-old female "eagler" as a houseguest. But I had waited to see that eagle and that fox converge for a long time. I had envisioned the scene in dreams, waking and sleeping. You might say it took me three years to see it in real life. But it might be more accurate to say that it took me forty-five.

MONGOLIA IS A LAND OF HISTORY AND DREAMS. FEAR OF THE horsemen from the mountains beyond the steppes shaped European culture. The name of Chingiz Khan is still a synonym for the conqueror, for the leader of hordes beyond civilization. America lived through a brief fascination with its plains and deserts in the twenties when Roy Chapman Andrews, the prototype for Indiana Jones, discovered the bones and the first eggs of dinosaurs in the Flaming Cliffs of the Gobi Desert, ushering in the first dinosaur craze.

But most Americans seem to have forgotten Mongolia and its people, its Buddhist Mongols, Moslem Kazakhs, and shamanist reindeer herders. A well-educated man in his fifties, with a degree from Washington and Lee University, asked me whether it was in the northern or southern hemisphere. Even those who know it is in the northern will ask me "What country is it in?" or assume that it is part of Russia, or China. Not a few have assumed that its government is hostile, communist, anti-American. Sometimes, when I contest these beliefs, I get the feeling that my listeners don't believe me.

Mongolia is as far away from the United States as a country can be, on the other side of the globe, between Siberia and China. It is spindle-shaped, pointed at both ends like a football. Superimposed on North America, it would extend from the borders of British Columbia and Alberta in the north to nearly touch Oklahoma in the south. Its western tip, which makes an X-shaped four corners with Siberia to the north, China to the south, and Kazakhstan just touching it in the west, would reach to eastern Washington state; its eastern point, bordering China's "Inner Mongolia," would be just above western New York. Ulaan Bataar, the capitol, would be near Chicago.

In the center of the largest continent, it would probably have a colder climate than the US even if it were lower, but its average height above sea level is 1,580 meters, more than five thousand feet—one of the highest average elevations in the world. Its highest peak, Tavanbogd Uul in the far west, stretches to 14,346 feet. Although most people who know it at all think of it as an endless grassy plain, the north is a landscape of well-watered hills and larch forest blending into spruce-fir taiga near Siberia. The far south is desert, and the far west dry mountains like New Mexico or Afghanistan.

It has relatively few inhabitants, and, as in America's rural west, everybody seems to know everybody else. It has more livestock than people. For every Mongolian it is estimated that there is one horse, 1.4 cows, four goats, and six sheep. There are enough camels in the south and west to equal the number of horses.

Mongolians spent sixty years under communism, much of it under the brutal thumb of Stalin's disciple Choibalsan who, among his other sins, tried to kill every Buddhist monk in the country. They now sometimes seem to resemble a nation of free-market anarchists, puzzled by America's rules and regulations. This is in part a reaction, in part an illusion; their community ethics and almost mystical love for the land are forces just as strong. But nomads have always valued freedom, and Mongolia has always been a society of nomads. Choibalsan's first attempt at collective agriculture failed when rural residents killed their livestock rather than submit. Even under the stifling bureaucracy that succeeded Choibalsan's tyranny and lasted until what Mongolians call "The Change" in 1990, nomads were largely exempt. It is hard to govern people you can't find.

This strange land has become familiar to me over the past few years. Walking the city of Ulaan Bataar and the rocky hills of Bayaan Olgii sometimes feels like coming home. I feel as though I know the streets of Ulaan Bataar as well as those of the Boston of my youth, and maybe even better than those of Santa Fe; I can lead you to Chapman's dinosaurs and the terrible claws of Deinocheirus, to the bookshop in the old State Department store, to a good Chinese restaurant, the best new bar, the cheapest cashmere store. I know which bank has the clock with the sculpture of the coelocanth on top (though I don't have the slightest idea why a Mongolian bank should display a rediscovered fossil fish from Africa.)

Returning to the scenes, smells, and tastes of Mongolia can give me a pang of recognition now, and encountering them elsewhere evokes a peculiar homesickness. The sweet toxic tang of coal smoke, smell of both my earliest youth and of winter in Ulaan Bataar, evokes the acid taste of hardened curd, that staple of every nomadic household, and the pleasant mix of smells that dung smoke and cooking a fat sheep make after a cold day's hunting. I can see a golden hill backed by a thundering black sky, a snow squall streaming down the rocky side of a mountain toward me, or a distant line of grazing beasts; see them in New Mexico or Montana, and be transported back instantly to a valley under white crags near the Siberian border.

Other things have no counterparts where I live, but still seem familiar whenever I see them again, whether over there or in a photo: white *gers*, the felt tents that Russians and Americans call yurts, clustered like mushrooms under a mountain's wall; great dark Bactrian camels grazing in green pasture along a meandering river under white crags, creatures left over from the Pleistocene; black choughs, like little ravens with bright red bills, whistling and diving over a remote adobe homestead twelve miles from the nearest tree; a flock of hill pigeons swirling in perfect synchronized harmony, their white tails flashing against lava rock. Above all, those domestic eagles, sitting stolidly in the remote side yards of the Kazakhs' "winter-spending places," calmer by far than any shaggy guard dog until they fly.

Even at home, in my flat-roofed house that would not seem out of place in Olgii, some rooms evoke the other side of the world. Walls are hung with vivid Islamic hangings, floors covered with felt rugs. Mongol snuff bottles battle for space with animal skulls and mementos from other journeys. A Mongolian bill, a *tugrug*, the paper currency of the country, is stuck to my bulletin board with a thumbtack; if I pick it up and sniff it, I can still smell mutton fat. Each time I return I see constant changes alongside the things that never change. I love its paradoxes, its space and hospitality, its freedom and ancient customs. It is a place of great roadless areas, all known and inhabited since prehistory. It is wild enough for great horned sheep; wolves, snow leopards, and the last undomesticated camels; with the lowest human population density on earth, but not a wilderness in the American sense. Nomads' flocks graze in its national parks, one of which is the oldest on earth. It is the home of Buddhist hunters and Moslems who toast their guests with vodka. I can't get enough of it, and probably never will.

But no more than five years ago it was as strange to me, as unreal and legendary, as it is still to most westerners; a place out of myth, fable, deep history; a place composed of images from musty old books, faded black-and-white-photographs; of dreams and yearning.

This book is about a dream that became real.

PART I

Dream

I saw a picture once, in a book I have forgotten, in an old city neighborhood of three-decker wooden tenements I may never visit again. I heard stories there, and saw animals: real ones, images in books, and ones I made in my head from the words in the stories.

My parents made images then. My father was an artist turned civil engineer and draftsman; my mother, a commercial fashion artist. Now I make stories for a living, and live with other animals around me. Fur-hatted nomads, horsemen from shining mountains, gallop through my flickering brain at night, while great birds soar and dive overhead. Some are dreams, where they mix with animals and people from Africa, or New Mexico. Some are memories.

Another memory: My mother in the yellow light at the foot of my bed, on a sweltering midsummer night, reading to me from a pretty new edition of Kipling's *Jungle Book:* the first story, "Mowgli's Brothers." There's the baby, fleeing through a night no darker than the one outside my window; the terrifying presence of Sher Khan, looming in the cave's mouth; the green-eyed defending demon of Raksha, Mowgli's wolf foster-mother, backing him away. Surely I create these from later readings? But I still have the book, marked and stained by childhood meals, and the memories of those characters are as real to me as those of the black coal chute in the cellar, the smell of it burning blue coal in the stove, the popped paper caps of frozen milk bottles on the back stoop, the cries of the ragman *("Rags and Bones! Rags and Bones!")* as he passed on the street with his horse-drawn wagon—all those fragments of another lost world.

That was in 1953, in Dorchester, a blue-collar neighborhood in Boston. In New Mexico nights, on the edge of sleep, the images still come to me, not in flashes nor in orderly narratives, but in sensory bursts like a kind of natural virtual reality. Do I pull them up out of the lightless well in my head, or create them out of still-tinier fragments because they are appropriate? Or did they build molecular structures in my developing brain, because they meant something important?

Words, images, animals. In 1953 I was already, improbably, fascinated by animals. They were so scarce I can remember each individual: a mouse that drowned in my bedside glass; a nest of sparrows that blew down from the eaves in a hurricane; my cousin's cat, Snoozy, who lived briefly upstairs and was run over by a car; the ragman's cart horse, which in 1953 still made the rounds every week.

It was probably no accident, given the neighborhood, that most of these were dead. More lively animals ran through the colorful magazines that my parents brought home. My parents told me I learned to read by matching the names of animals under the fold-out dioramas in *Life* to their owners: weasel, fox, deer, blue jay. I can recall, a little later, matching the head of a jaguar on the cover of some glossy color magazine to the word "sports" in the magazine's title, except that I, understandably, thought the word was "spots."

It was in a magazine that I first saw The Picture. No amount of mental searching can bring back the name of the particular magazine, nor could my parents recall it; they thought, I suspect, that most of my earliest memories are hallucinations, though I can still startle my mother by imitating the rag man, or by remembering that the landlord's name was Mr. Mahan.

The first incarnation is a full-page illustration. A man sits astride a pale gray horse. He is brown-skinned, squinting, with a fur hat on his head. He has a thin mustache and a spike of beard, and wears a coat of pale fur, almost white, marked with black rosettes, that resembles a rougher, grayer version of my mother's ocelot coat, the one she was given when she was the illustrator for a Newbury Street furrier. In retrospect, I am sure that it is made from snow leopard.

But even the splendid coat, even better than my mother's (along with the iridescent blue wing feathers of the ducks my father shot, two totems of almost fetishistic intensity when I was young), pales beside what the man carries. His arm, sheathed in heavy leather, resembles a tree trunk. On it stands a bird nearly as large as the man. It is black and gold, with a great curving hook of a beak, and it is looking at me.

I try and try to remember exactly what I asked as I stared at this wonderful picture. All I can remember is what my mother tells me, at least a bit accurately. The man is "a Russian." The bird is a golden eagle.

GIVEN THE TIMES AND THE PLACE—THE COLD WAR, CATHOLIC Boston—it's a small miracle that the word "Russian" did not make me push the image away rather than make it an icon that still haunts me. Instead, it became one of a small set of triggers, stimuli that pulled me away from the mainstream, made me live more familiarly in alien worlds than the one I was born in, pulled me toward strange journeys, poverty, hardship, and delight.

For the next ten, twenty, forty years, through various transmutations of national politics, opinions, interests, versions of myself, I would encounter The Picture. It was not always the same photo, of course; I never saw the original hunter in snow leopard again. It became a multitude, a horseback army of Asian nomads, scanned and printed on my brain over forty years, taken over a much longer span than that. Some were dim halftone plates in old travel books, now "de-accessioned," that once inhabited the vaults of the Ames Free Library in Easton, where we moved from Dorchester. One of the more recent, a three-by-five transparency, was handed to me by the woman who took it, a Russo-Hungarian entrepreneur who lived in a high-rise over Brighton Beach. There are dozens on my desk.

Their backgrounds may be blurred, or snow-white and featureless. If they are in color, the sky is often that vivid dark blue common to high-altitude dry plains from New Mexico to the Altai range. In Carruther's *Beyond the Caspian,* written in the twenties and thirties but published in 1948, there is a line of smudges, like a horizontal smoke signal, on the horizon. In Owen Lattimore's 1930 *High Tartary,* long, hard-edged sunset shadows stretch across the figures and into the distance. Behind the image of a boy with an eagle in Clara Szklarz's transparency squats the formerly Soviet space shuttle, piggybacked on an enormous jet. In a photo clipped from *World Monitor,* bare brown hills like those north of my house in New Mexico rise to frame the characters. In the scholarly *Nomads of Eurasia,* they are backed by a grove of very Russian birches. In two reproductions of a Kazakh calendar, sent to me from New Orleans and Russia, there is nothing but Xerox gray behind them.

In a magical painting by the Russian-born Taos artist Leon Gaspard, who traveled the caravan routes for years, the nomad is transformed into "Prince Igor" in a robe decorated with blood-red poppies and pink roses. But his eagle, properly supported by the birchwood crutch called a *baldach,* wears what I would learn was a Kazakh hood.

Over a span of seventy-some years, however different the backgrounds, the character remains the same. He has brown skin turned to leather by the wind, Asian eyes slit against the glare; high cheekbones. He might have a thin mustache, or a chin beard. He looks a little like an American Indian, perhaps a Navajo. He is almost always wearing a round wolfskin hat, with flaps over his ears. He also wears a knee-length wool cloak, with or without a broad belt ornamented with silver, a heavy engraved silver ring on his finger like those made in the pueblos, tall boots trimmed with fur. There's a dagger in his belt, a rifle slung across his shoulder. He's mounted on a horse.

On his fist, always, stands the eagle. Usually her great brown eyes are covered by a helmet-shaped hood, an eyeless mask sometimes decorated with silver or crusts of gold braid. She always looks as big as he does. She (female eagles are invariably bigger than males) is as black as a hole in the night.

IN MY CHILDHOOD, I HAD NO MENTOR TO TEACH ME ABOUT birds or far places. But I had the next best thing: old books. In the fifties, the town of Easton was graced with an unusual public library. The Ames family, shovel manufacturers turned to squires by money and time, had commissioned the architect H. H. Richardson to build them a groined neo-medieval vault, and filled it with a treasure trove of books. That library bent my life for good.

By 1959, I read well enough to be allowed up into the dim stacks of the adult section, where all the really good stuff was. It was there that I first read Darwin, a nineteenth-century edition of *The Variation of Plants and Animals Under Domestication* with its feather-perfect Victorian steel engravings of pigeons. I sampled William Beebe, who traveled to the Galapagos and the Himalayas and descended to the depths of the ocean in his bathysphere, and who wrote of the wilds of Burma where, collecting pheasants, he met and photographed, "The shooter of poisoned arrows," laconically adding under the caption: "From the hillside just behind, he shot at us for three nights. The evening following this photograph, I shot and killed him. See page 127."

It was there I found The Picture for my first conscious time. In another travel book, Douglas Carruther's *Beyond the Caspian,* is a slightly blurred black-and-white photo of a horseman. On his fist stands—"perches" is far too small, almost effete, a word—the same great black eagle. Her amazingly small head is turned toward the man's face, but hooded. A loop or thong, incongruously like an antenna, sprouts from its crown. Beneath the photo, a simple inscription, "Berkut or Kush."

The text, the first I had read on the eagles, was amazing.

". . . The quarry consists mostly of foxes, gazelle, wolves, and in earlier days, the Saiga antelope. Some authorities, Levchine for instance, declare that if a wolf is too strong, and goes off with the eagle still hanging on to it, the eagle is able to hold it with one foot and anchor itself with the other, until the wolf exhausts itself in the struggle! . . . eagles are [also] used at wild boar hunts." Carruthers—no sensationalist, but a sober British geographer and naturalist—goes on for several pages that combine observation and scholarly quibbles about what race the Kirghiz hunting eagle might be.

I never forgot that book. Ten years ago, I bought it—a small blue volume, about eight-by-five inches, with its title embossed in gold. It was published in 1949, about expeditions made mostly in the first two decades of the century. I open it and inhale; its old-book smell is as evocative of dreams of far places as Proust's madeleine was of his past. When I was a child, I assumed I would go everywhere.

THOSE OF US WHO BECOME TRAVELERS SEEM TO LOCK INTO certain images early, the way young birds imprint on an image that becomes "mother." I love, theoretically, rain forests and jungles—their smells, intricacy, hallucinatory biodiversity, their birds and bugs. But something about bleak plains and sculpted rocks, Himalayan crags, slant-eyed horsemen in fur hats, turned in my developing brain the way a key does in a lock. As I progressed through grade school I read books of adventure and travel from all over the world, but the images that stayed with me were the ones from Roy Chapman Andrews, Peter Fleming, and the *Kim* of Kipling, from adventure novels by Talbot Mundy, kid's books about Chingiz Khan, photos of Afghanistan, tales of fossil digs in the Gobi Desert. I wanted to travel on horse and camel-back, under cold dry mountains that stood above endless vistas of blue and red, through valleys full of enigmatic stuff—old tombs and crumbling buildings, unreadable texts on canyon walls, stone monuments older than our civilization holding hints of meaning for those learned enough to decipher them. I wanted to see hairy beasts of burden, hunt wild sheep, roam amidst nomads, camels, and goats.

Such influences shape you in ways you may not understand until long after the path is taken, the choice made. Certainly they led me into falconry, a pursuit so odd in my ethnic and suburban background that, though it became a focus of my life at about eleven, I did not find a mentor for ten years, despite writing letters to anyone who seemed to have the remotest connection with the sport. I trapped my first hawk at thirteen. I have been at it ever since.

And looking back, what on earth led me to New Mexico twenty years ago? It too has the mountains, plains, vistas, dry air, ruins, horsemen, and petroglyphs, though I considered my arrival there more of an accident than a plan. I found something else in New Mexico that I had yearned for in my dreams, something that barely existed in New England: an unsentimental intimacy with, and a life lived among, animals; not a sentimental animal rights view of them, nor a reduction of them to utilitarian automatons, but a kind of familiarity with them that acknowledged that they were not humans but that they were persons, whether part of the family, servants, friends, or enemies.

Some reporters think that Spanish and Moslem cultures are cruel to animals, or that they see them as ends. The late Italian mountaineer and cross-cultural explorer Fosco Maraini said that in what he calls "prophetic" cultures like Islam, ". . . animals are excluded in participation in the cosmic drama. . . . They are living creatures, nothing more." I can only speak for the people I have known, but high-desert people were the first I ever met who accepted animals unselfconsciously into the community as important actors and participants. If you read the novels of Central Asia's greatest modern writer, the Kirghiz Chingiz Aitmatov, you will find that his horses and wolves (and Christ, and Pilate) are just as real and developed characters as his members of the Russian Mafia, or his human protagonists. It is a way of life that northern Europeans are steadily leaving behind.

I wanted this intimacy, and have sought it out in places and people, from backcountry New England trappers, field zoologists, pigeon flyers, falconers, horsemen, dog trainers, cowboys, Indians, and whoever else would teach me and talk to me. I looked for it in books, too, especially old ones. It seemed to me that in Central Asia there was much to be learned, from falconers, sure, but also from Buddhists and Sufis and breeders of ancient lines of horses and dogs, of Akhal-Tekes, Tazis, and Taighans. But finally, you can get lost in all the books and all the dusty branching byways of history. You realize that you will have to go yourself, to *do,* else the whole picture becomes a mere tangle in the neurons in your head.

THE BIRDS, AND EVEN THE DEEP TRAIL OUR RELATIONS WITH them has worn in human culture—the falconry "meme"—are as real as rock. Eagles have been connected to humans for a long time. Roger Tory Peterson said that man emerged from the mists of prehistory "with a peregrine perched on his fist . . . ," romantic and at least half true. Falconry is older than our civilization. The sweet elegant little peregrine is a toy for developed cultures, but the first falconers were practical. Such tribes as the Bedouin or the Kazakhs praise and prize their birds, but scorn prey that is neither edible nor commercial. Eagles, with a greater need for food than small falcons, with life spans of thirty and forty years, must have paid their way. The oldest falconry cultures, the ones that seem to descend unbroken from the time when horses were tamed, are eagle cultures. It would make more metaphoric sense to speak of mankind, riding out of the steppes of Central Asia with an eagle perched before him in the saddle.

The eagle known to most old societies was the golden eagle, "the" eagle, *aetus,* the aquila of the Romans, the "damn black Mexican eagle" of border sheepmen. Golden eagles, at least those of some races, are among the three or four largest predatory birds in the world, and perhaps the most biologically successful. They live clear across North America, from Labrador to Mexico, in Siberia, across Asia and Europe, and down into the mountains of Morocco. Close relations inhabit South Africa and Australia. They are the bird of prey with the closest relations to humans—antagonistic and utilitarian, mythical and real, even theological—for uncounted thousands of years. Golden eagles are actors in Pueblo Indian rituals; their tail feathers are sacred to the Plains tribes. The ancient Romans, who gave the name *Aquila* to the species and later to the genus, used them as battle standards and war animals that could attack the heads of their enemies. They were reserved for emperors in European falconry, and are still used to hunt wolves in Central Asia and deer in eastern Europe. They have been poisoned by Scottish sheepherders, accused of stealing babies, and hunted from single-engine airplanes in Texas as recently as the early sixties. Contrary to the assertions of some of their more sentimental defenders, they are capable of taking antelope and deer in the wild, and, at least once, have been proven to kill calves.

These days predators, in the popular imagination, are seen as utterly benign creatures. Think of *The Lion King*, where prey animals appear as counselors to the hero. What do they think that lions eat? In such an atmosphere, it's hard to resist quoting the old Canadian trapper who caught wolves for the Yellowstone restoration project, who said, "Ranchers think that wolves live on cows, and environmentalists think they live on mice; they're both full of shit." Our imagination fails to comprehend other animals in two ways. On the one hand, we dismiss them as a mass of insentient beings who react to stimuli and do not think—Cartesian automatons. On the other, we clothe human minds in different costumes, in feathers and fur and scales. We need new ways of imagining the minds of the "other bloods" with whom we share our world. Golden eagles contain power and intelligence in a body that weighs only twelve pounds. They can appear and disappear like magic in seconds, fall out of the sky at one hundred miles per hour to kill a hundred-pound antelope or a five-pound flying goose with no tools, only the muscles of a hollow-boned body smaller than a child's. Aquila's talons can exert tons of pressure at their tips. Her great brown eyes, capable of resolving a pigeon's wing-flick at two miles, weigh more than her intelligent brain.

ON A JANUARY DAY A FEW WINTERS BACK, A BIOLOGIST FRIEND and a companion were testing their skills calling coyotes in the Red Desert. The word "desert" may call to mind a hot, dry place full of cacti and colorful rocks. Though it can be hellishly hot in summer, the Red Desert of Wyoming is less picturesque. It consists of that stretch of Wyoming that most tourists hustle through as fast as possible on the interstate: the flat part between Laramie and the high hills on the Utah border, south of the Wind River Range, north of Colorado's shining mountains. It is part of the Basin and Range geological province and mostly consists, to the casual observer, of sagebrush and alkali. In the winter, temperatures there can reach forty below zero. Some creatures do live there—a few scattered cattle, some herds of sheep. Some even flourish: antelope, coyotes, prairie rattlesnakes, sage grouse, prairie falcons, golden eagles. For those who love harsh desolate places and their fine-tuned inhabitants, the Red Desert is a place of revelations and marvels.

That day, the hunter's persistent calling had gone unanswered. It was mid-morning under a solid gray sky, on the third day of a hard freeze, and at ten the temperature had still not risen above twenty-six below. The biologist and his friend, giving up on staying warm under a sheet of snow camouflage, had decided to pack up. Then the friend noticed an odd movement a half mile away, at the bottom of the slight rise of land upon which they were perched. A group of antelope had bunched up and started to run.

"It was weird. It was like they were fish or something. They weren't just milling around, either—they were coordinated. They'd all run one way, then all run around together and run the other way."

Then he saw the bird, way off to one side of the sky. "It was an eagle, a big old black female. She was flapping hard to stay up—no thermals on a day like that, no wind, remember. And I say 'Haa—if we didn't know better, I'd swear she was stalking those antelope.'

"And then she just turned over and stooped at them like a giant peregrine."

As she plunged into the terrified herd, it exploded in all directions. "For a second there you couldn't see anything. They busted up like a school of fish that you dropped a rock on, and there was snow flying all over the place. Then all of a sudden they were all gone except for one. And the eagle was hanging on its neck."

The antelope didn't seem able to run. He walked in slow circles, as the eagle balanced herself, flapping and, as the observers could see through their binoculars, shifting and kneading with her feet. "He was hunched up like a cat on a fence, with his head down—like he was gut-shot."

At that moment a complication entered the picture, stage left. The coyote that they had been calling vainly all morning appeared in the middle distance, running straight at the combatants. All

predators are opportunists, and in conditions as drastic as a prolonged freeze they will be drawn to any commotion. This coyote
went running straight at the eagle and the antelope. "He got about
fifty feet away and the eagle took off. The antelope took off too, but
I don't think it did him any good. He ran by us so close we could
hear him breathing, with the coyote right behind him. Arterial
blood was shooting out three feet to one side. Steam was boiling off
his wounds like it was a tea kettle."

I sat amazed; I knew that eagles could theoretically tackle such
large quarry, but this was my first eyewitness account. Finally I asked
whether he thought that the attack was brought on by the extreme
conditions. He hesitated a moment. He is a scientist, as he will tell
you, cautious about making outrageous statements. Finally, he shook
his head and grinned. "Naah," he said. "She knew exactly what she
was doing. It was like she did it *every fucking week.*"

Eagles are not "just like us." The sentimental belief that an animal with whom we feel affinity is like us (or worse, *likes* us) is not the
least of our cultural idiocies. It's probably easier to "understand"—
all these questions and approximations must be put in quotes once
you begin to think hard about them—easier to understand an insect
than an eagle. Insect senses and drives are far more alien, but their
behaviors are reflexive and mechanical; binary; on or off. Eagles
think and learn. But what to make of the mind of a creature, who, if
well-fed, will sit from dawn to dusk just watching? Or to whom it is
"moral" to kill her weaker sibling in the nest? Nobody but another
eagle could easily read a lifelike narrative of an eagle's life without
spasms of boredom or horror.

We are human, and so wish we could fly with eagles, hunt with
them like earthbound mates. This wish to understand, to know, and
even for a moment to be something different; or failing that, to speak
of it, is an entirely human wish; an eagle would not comprehend, nor

care. An eagle's perception of its own life might be of a bright eternal present, like a carnivorous Buddhist's—confident, centered, and watchful, with a dimmer past and no thought of the future. If she thought of us at all, she might think that we crawl on the earth, eating dirt and sticks, killing from afar with a loud noise if we manage to see our prey at all. If she could speak, she might say, like Ted Hughes's "Hawk Roosting," "I hold creation in my foot / or fly up, and revolve it all slowly—I kill where I please because it is all mine . . . Nothing has changed since I began."

I BECAME A FALCONER IN THE SIXTIES, AND MADE MY FIRST attempt to train an eagle in '71. She broke my hand.

Falconry is a peculiar kind of biophilia. T. H. White, writing about it in the thirties, called it "a sort of mania." At its best—or, some disgruntled falconers' partners might say, its worst—it combines in a seamless whole birding, hunting, and animal (I will not say "pet") keeping, but it goes one step further. Kent Carnie, now director of the archives at the North American Center for Birds of Prey, put it most simply: "You are the bird." When it works, it almost seems like you, the human partner, are flying, rolling, diving, seeing through those inhumanly perfect eyes. It is addictive and thrilling, even in its more savage aspects. To quote White, a gentle man who understood his mania, again: "Blood lust is a word that has got shop soiled. They have rubbed the nap off it. But split it into its parts, and think of lust."

When I acquired my first and only eagle, I had flown redtails, easygoing rabbit hawks that were forgiving of human mistakes, and the more difficult and nervy goshawks, who, despite their fundamentally deranged personalities, are still favorites of mine. It was a kind of apprenticeship under the wings of my partners. But I was a long way from being a bird; I was just a newly divorced part-time night zookeeper, living in a converted chicken coop with star maps on the wall. She was a steppe or tawny eagle from the plains of Eurasia, a smaller relative of the golden, rescued from servitude as a college mascot under conditions that are illegal now and should have been back then. Her "duty" had been to accompany a pair of buzz-headed fraternity oafs to football games, where she and her mate hung screaming from their hockey gloves. Between games, they were boarded in a cement-floored perchless cage in a local zoo and fed something euphemistically called "raptor chow": whole ground turkeys stuffed into plastic tubes, like immense frozen breakfast sausages. After the male died, some nameless friends helped me disappear the female into my kinder hands. Of course, she hated me as much as she hated everybody else.

The talons on her short yellow toes, after two years on concrete, looked more like knitting needles than scimitars. So when I decided to rehabilitate her, I didn't worry much. I couldn't even feel my goshawk's sharp claws through the welder's glove I pulled on. But when I tried to withdraw a bit of food through my fist, she glared at me and squeezed. Pain, like a drawn-out hammer blow, knocked me to me knees. My then-girlfriend, who liked my hawks better than she liked me, thought this was hilarious. I lay on the grass and moaned, then asked her to light me a cigarette. I smoked unfiltered Camels then, and still can feel the distracting bite of the smoke, my gritted teeth, the unbelievable pressure on my hand. Three smokes later the bird relented, unlocked her feet, and bounded back to her perch with a single flap. When I eased my hand out of the glove I could see no breaks in the skin, only white spots. The ER doctor found two cracks in the small bones behind my knuckles. Learning afterward that eagles develop several tons of pressure at their talon tips was a small, belated, intellectual consolation. She went to a friend's breeding project, where she still lives thirty years later.

⌒⏤⏤⏤

AT ABOUT THE SAME TIME THAT I HAD THAT COLLISION, A chance reading of the memoirs of an elderly eagle-trainer brought the idea of The Picture back into my conscious dreaming. F. W. Remmler was not just an eccentric old man with pet eagles. He was the Eagle-Man, the only falconer in the English-speaking world with a direct line to the nomads in Central Asia, a man who had killed wolves with birds, a man whose perches were made before World War I by the Kirghiz on his first visit to what he always called "the Kirghizian Steppe."

When Remmler was born, in 1888, he was already an anachronism. Falconry in the West had become a mannered pastime of a few scholarly aristocrats who preferred to use peregrines instead of shotguns. Even goshawks were considered coarse; Sir John Sebright, the Victorian polymath who allegedly caught a partridge with a Sparrowhawk ten days after he captured it, and who "invented" breeds of chicken and pigeon, sneered that he "never could understand how any one could use these birds for sport."* Eagles were worse. Those few (mostly Russian) Europeans who knew of the Asian eagle-men

---

* John Cummins, in his scholarly *The Hound and the Hawk,* quotes the fourteenth-century writer Gace de la Vigne on "austringers," those who fly goshawks and other coarse birds: ". . . please do not house your graceless austringers in the falconer's room. They are cursed in Scripture, for they hate company and go alone about their sport. . . When one sees an ill-formed man, with great big feet . . . hump-shouldered and skew-backed, and one wants to mock him, one says, 'Look, what an austringer!' I know the austringers would like to beat me for this, but there are two dozen of us falconers to one of them, so I have no fear."

considered them barbarians and primitives, both legendary and vaguely disreputable.

A few romantics dissented. Apparently some enterprising Russian brought "Mongols"—probably actually Kazakhs or Kirghiz—to the Tolstoy estate in 1856, to fly at wolves in celebration of the accession of Czar Alexander II. The English setter breeder William Humphrey, like many eagle-men a semi-legendary character for other reasons than his eagle, practically invented the modern English field setter. Between the 1890s and the 1920s he kept a golden that killed hundreds of foxes in the wild hill-country of Wales, after his dogs pointed them. But he didn't write about it, so only fragmentary accounts remain. A few showmen, then and now, have tamed eagles and used them in displays. But the secrets of how to fly them like wild hunters seemed lost to the West, holding on only in the shadows of the Tien Shan and Altai ranges, close to the forbidden missile fields, spaceports, and nuclear test sites of the former Soviet Union.

But just before that late empire walled the eagle people away from Western eyes, Remmler got in. One of God's own autocrats, he was born to rule, and never doubted himself or his privileges. He wrote: "I have persevered in the traditions all my life and have never veered from this path. Already as a young boy, I would have been a match for any Prussian nobleman or Baltic baron." Reading his *Reminisces*, a passionate, detailed, rambling document in an original version of English that was published privately in 1970, the modern reader might wonder how anyone so arrogant could simultaneously be so humble before nature.

The paradox is in the mind of the reader. Accepted political dualities of left and right have nothing to do with Remmler, who lived in an already-past time that predated such distractions. He was a Teutonic Knight, an absolute elitist who hunted wolves and foxes with eagles and who would keep up to sixteen at a time, not to mention a support staff of servants, horses, and hounds. He always kept a pair of wolverines as house pets. His pronouncements were medieval. "Whoever has ridden hundreds of horses or has hunted with hounds will agree that no two animals are exactly alike, just as this is rarely the case with human beings. Only lame-brains and world do-gooders preach of the category, without believing a moment themselves, that all men are the same."

Remmler trained his first eagle (brought to him by tenants on the family estate) in 1905. He worked out how to house, train, and fly it on his own before he ever met the eagle tribes. "It was clear to me how things should be handled," he wrote, although he adds, "I had already been hunting with eagles for about ten years before I finally learned how I was supposed to carry and fly a hunting bird in the traditional manner." He was seventeen.

His uncle worked for Alfred Nobel's oil company and had interests in the Caucasus and "Kirghizia," so it was inevitable that he would travel to the steppes, to seek out mentors in the ancient horse cultures that he came to respect with the same intensity with which he despised the modern world. His perspective was not without humor, though: "The Kirghizian had many likeness [*sic*] to the modern Americans. They rode their horses even when the distance was scarcely 100 paces and the Americans today climb in their vehicles to go about the same distance."

Remmler fought in the German army in both World Wars and ended up in an American POW camp. The Russians wanted him dead or alive as a war criminal, but General Motors Corporation brought him to Canada to run its immense hunting preserve on an island in Lake Erie. He lived out his life in Canada with wolverines and eagles, never surrendering an inch to a Cold War world he considered equally corrupt on both sides. In his memoirs, he calls American game management "communistic" and quotes a Kirghiz nomad:

"I asked the man if he would ever leave his homeland. The Kirghiz, who spoke Russian, got on his horse, made a sweeping gesture which Napoleon would have been able to envy and said 'Leave this land? Has not Allah given us the steppe? Who is the measure of whether the gift of God is enough or not?' This man was a hunter by God's grace, and my teaching mentor."

Here he is on his favorite bird. "I pictured this one as a wolf eagle. After she had her basic training behind her, I began training her for the hunt and indeed only for wolves. A woman animal care-taker at my farm had a twelve-year old son, who was very small, who played the wolf. A true artist in leather work . . . made him some armor out of strong leather. On the back of this was laid a wolf pelt with a large piece of meat tied to it. The first practice was in the area near the perch, since all hunting birds show more courage at home than in the field. As the boy loped [past] my eagle, she struck him immediately. I grabbed the bird quickly and set her on the perch and gave her the meat from the back of the boy."

And yet, Remmler, whom you can easily imagine riding after his quarry over terrified peasants' grain fields, sickened so suddenly of his beloved wolf hunting that he called off an expensive expedition halfway through, buying off his disgruntled and disappointed employees with cases of vodka. He would later write: "The wolf should not be caught, poisoned, hunted with birds, shot or trapped."

One might dismiss this as sentimentality, the flip side of cruelty. But Remmler knew more lasting truths about sport and art and life. He counsels the aspiring falconer to take his time and ease: "Finally one hunts for the pleasure, and is called out of love for art, not in order to set some record or make a drudgery out of it. If someone likes to toil, there are many activities where this has more place. For myself, personally, I have no need for drudgery, records, or what have you of any sort. Therefore, if one is in a hurry, he might as well lay this book aside and start reading one of the many textbooks on falconry, just as thick as the ones on war and peace."

I DID NOT PARTICULARLY WANT TO KILL A FOX, NEVER MIND A wolf; I had and have a tender, probably too sentimental, identification with predators. When, fifteen years later, I saw a pack of splendid greyhounds light out after a coyote, all I could think of was how much the fleeing canid reminded me of my little "Indian dog" back home. I cheered when she escaped, even though one of the greyhounds was mine. But *I wanted to be in The Picture.* I wanted to live that whole life. And if the price were the life of a wolf, so be it. It seemed a remote possibility. All the ancient bird cultures, the Kazakhs, and Kirghiz, and Turkmens, were locked behind an impenetrable political barrier; no English speakers had traveled among them since Carruthers and the blacklisted scholar-adventurer Owen Lattimore.

Meanwhile, I would travel any distance to see a working bird. In 1971 a big female golden belonging to a friend in upstate New York leaped off its perch at me like a junkyard dog; fortunately, her leash stopped her six inches short of my foot. Shortly thereafter, on a training flight, she killed a neighbor's chicken. When her owner went in to take her up, she bristled and mantled, shielding her prey with her wings. He ignored her and squatted, talking to her, crooning her name. She came up and in a quick strike locked one foot just above his ankle and one on his inner thigh, just missing his femoral artery. A friend managed to pry her off, after a few long moments. When the falconer got out of the hospital, he found that he could not await her coming in without flinching. He gave her to a wildlife refuge where she remains today, still unpredictable, too dangerous to release.

The trouble was that none of us knew eagle technique. Not everything that worked on hawks would work on eagles. All birds are more "other" than dogs and cats, never mind chimps; this otherness is simply a measure of how long ago our evolving paths diverged. But in the smaller raptors, their simpler minds and quick metabolism, together with the necessary opportunism that is part of the hardwiring of predators, made them easy to train. They learn almost immediately that humans have food. Despite legends to the contrary, you don't have to starve them, just show them food when they are hungry, food in your hand. It's like training a dog with biscuits. Once they learn that you not only feed them but can make their prey break cover, the bond is sealed. Although the nuances are endless (and clumsiness can ruin progress) the process is fundamentally as simple as that.

But eagles are not quite that simple. (Konrad Lorenz thought differently, saying that "all birds of prey are, compared with passerines or parrots, extremely stupid creatures." He based this authoritative statement on one four-year old captive that had never been flown before he acquired her, and that he soon gave to a zoo.) Part of their complexity, I suspect, is that they are a lot bigger than other birds of prey. More size—a female golden is twice the size of the next biggest American hawk, the ferruginous—implies more brain cells, more connections, more complexity. It means that hunger is no longer as dominant a stimulus; eagles voluntarily fast for up to a month a year. Finally, eagles are long-lived predators, living over forty years; in fact one of the longest-lived predators on earth, whether bird or mammal. This implies memory, learning, the ability to make subtle distinctions.

Eagles must be wooed, not hurried, and handled with extreme care. Ones raised from birth are more likely to develop both aggression and "crushes" than ones taken at one to three years old. Eagles older than that can be so set in their ways they almost never learn trust. Making them very hungry can make them savage and possessive, but when they are very fat they are sluggish and content, unwilling to fly across the yard.

Females dominate the males and may challenge your dominance; they can weigh almost twice as much as males, and are far more dangerous. Until recently, the few Westerners who flew eagles preferred agile six-pound males to twelve-pound females, although the females can take such huge quarry as wolf, and are used on such quarry as deer by a new group of falconers in Eastern Europe. Some seemingly reputable English eaglers even insist that females need "discipline" in the form of, say, a whack with a rolled newspaper, when they struggle to dominate their trainer. Such a concept seems utterly perverse to this falconer; the one thing you never do is raise your voice or your hand to your bird. Besides, I might hesitate to threaten anything that can kill wolves, and fly.

WITH THE END OF THE SOVIET UNION, THE WALL AROUND the countries east of Russia had disappeared, and two American falconers, Eric Ratering and Richard Lowery, forwarded comments and material from Russian scientists and falconers; Lowery could also translate. The material was wonderful, some of the assumptions across cultures more difficult. Several of the Russians thought I could pay them five-figure amounts to publish their manuscripts in the US and even provide and pay for a translator. I got photos of eagles catching foxes and roe deer, scholarly essays by the ornithologist Sasha Sorokin, and such oddities as pieces of calendars and articles from Russian hunting magazines on coursing dogs. And, of course, dozens of variations on The Picture.

But the best of all these good things was a Russian-English falconry glossary. It was done in pencil by a Russian falconer with a little English, to while away the time while snowed in on a hawk-trapping expedition to Siberia, and kindly sent to me by Richard Lowery. It consists of four detailed pages. The meaning is clear, the language touching, the falconer's knowledge of his subject obvious. It also gives a whole new sinister meaning to the word tidbit, one that has enjoyed a certain vogue among my friends since then.

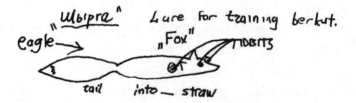

It wasn't quite as bad as it looked—the inverted commas around the word "fox" were explained on the next page as meaning that you used a fox *skin*. But it would probably be naive to expect Western notions of animal rights to have infected Central Asia; despite the nomads' kindness to their eagles and horses, they had never been known for loving their adversaries.

AS YOU MIGHT GUESS, THERE ARE ONLY A FEW AMERICAN eagle flyers. Although federal regulations theoretically allow falconers to possess and fly eagles, individual bureaucrats have a well-documented history of foot-dragging on permits, of blocking access to eagles. The only Americans with decent access to these quite common birds (which until the seventies were shot from airplanes in Texas and which are still legally trapped and relocated by animal control agents) are state-sanctioned Native Americans, who kill twenty or thirty every year for religious ceremonies, suffocating them in cornmeal. Therefore, even the most law-abiding and punctilious eagle-falconers tend to keep a low profile. So, I'm going to refer to my next informant, one of the most accomplished (and possibly the most enthusiastic) American eaglers of my acquaintance, only as "Patrick," and say of him only that he lives in the Rocky Mountains.

In 1992 I got a letter from him. A schoolteacher who built fly rods on the side, he wanted to build me one at cost, in hope that I would like it and tell my friends. Although he and I were members of what *Hawk Chalk* magazine refer to as the "falconry community"—a village of fewer than 2,500 people, spread around forty-nine states—we hadn't met, nor did we know that we were both falconers.

I stopped by his place on my way to Montana a few months later, to ask him about one of his specialties, the uncommon ferruginous hawk of the high plains. He took me in and showed me his rod shop, his reptiles, his skull collection, bobcat, and goshawk.

A few whiskeys later, recovered from the road burn of the day, I asked Patrick about the eight-by-ten photo of an eagle perched on his stepson's crib that he had displayed on the wall. *"Eagles,"* he said. "Let me show you something." He went to a corner and rummaged around, returning in a moment with a T-shaped perch that socketed into a belt. "This is what's called a *krakel,"* he said. "It used to belong to this guy . . . have you ever heard of Frederick Remmler?"

I CAUGHT MY FIRST HAWK, A ROBIN-SIZED KESTREL, AT THIRTEEN. I used a bownet made out of badminton netting attached to two yardsticks. Patrick used a bicycle and a gunny sack. In every way, he started bigger.

On a winter day in 1964, an eight-year-old Patrick was stalking his quarry. In Stevensville, Ontario, just across the Canadian border from Buffalo, New York, Remmler kept his avian companions. Five golden eagles sat on blocks made of cross-sectioned tree trunks, a magnet for any boy who loved wild things. The birds were close beneath Remmler's windows, under his constant supervision. But a quarter mile away was a field with only one eagle, a huge female named Freya, who was kept separately because she hated the other birds. Patrick had watched the old man pass among his flock many times, giving them tidbits and murmuring endearments. They were not accessible, but Freya was.

Patrick tells the story to me. "*Freya*, man. She was great, huge, *mean*. Later I once saw her foot Remmler above his glove and lay a tendon bare." He shakes his head at the old man's stoicism. "You should have seen him—he just pops the tendon back in his arm, stroking her breast, saying 'pretty girl, beautiful girl.' Anyway, I've got this sack, and I'm over the fence. I'm planning to stick her in the sack like some chicken, and drive home on my bike. And, I guess, keep her in my room—you know, 'Hey Mom, I caught this eagle . . .' So I'm just about to her perch, and she's looking at me, and she's got her hackles up, her mouth open. If I ever saw an eagle looking at me like that today, I'd run inside and slam the door. And I hear this shout, and I look back, and I see Grandpa Remmler running at me as fast as he can.

"He's pretty fast for an old guy. Before I can figure out what to do he runs up and grabs me. Starts shaking me. He's not just mad, he's scared. He keeps shaking me and saying, 'Sonny, sonny—don't you know this bird can *hurt* you?'"

When Remmler dragged the boy inside and called his parents, a friendship and apprenticeship began. When he died, he left Patrick, the young thief from an America he barely deigned to notice, his perches and his glove: his eagle tools made for him so long ago, on the Kirghizian Steppe.

EVERY YEAR AROUND THANKSGIVING THE NORTH AMERICAN Falconer's Association sponsors a meeting somewhere in the West, in some place with open skies and plenty of game. Hundreds of falconers gather from all over the world to fly birds, eat and drink, swap tales and goods, and make what may be their only social contact of the year with others of their kind. It's great fun if you like that sort of thing. But I am unnerved by crowds (I missed Woodstock on purpose), and in twenty-five years of NAFA membership have successfully managed to miss every meet. Maybe I should have been to this one. After Patrick returned with gleeful tales of having finally met "The Russians," it took me until the next summer to make contact with them. Or, as it turned out, for them to find me.

Meanwhile, a lot of strange stories were circulating. When I asked some falconers who had been to the meet about the Russians, the Kazakhs, and the mysterious film, I heard nothing good. The Russians were greedy. The Kazakhs were barbarians. Their eagles were ragged, starved, with dull claws. The films were incompetent. No, they were good, but staged. No, staged and faked, *and* barbaric. The eagles in the films killed foxes, wolves, lynxes, deer. Eagles couldn't kill mammals that large with any competence. Yes, they could, but they shouldn't; large-mammal hawking was revolting, bloody, cruel, lacking in all merit. It was unsportsmanlike. It would reflect badly on the "falconry community" if anyone saw the movies. They should be repressed, or at least not encouraged. Why in hell did anybody want to fly an eagle anyway?

It sounded like the rhetoric of some extremist anti-hunting group—or like that of the English tabloid press. I had recently been sent a colorful photo essay from England on deer hunting with eagles, titled "A Death Too Cruel," that defined falconry as "the ruthless destruction of wildlife by birds of prey" and said of falconers that they "took delight in the pain and final tearing to pieces of kicking bodies." Eagles were "not the prettiest birds in the world" and were "sky sloths"; but Grizelda, the featured bird, was still capable of "homing in on her unfortunate prey at speeds of up to 60 mph." After explaining how she had been "skillfully trained to savage on sight, spilling blood on the snow-covered landscapes and tearing flesh from the very bones of her victims," the writer finished with a remarkable paragraph: "When eagles, like Grizelda, get locked on their prey, they've been known to fly straight into fences of high-voltage wires. And, according to some of the locals who hate the thought of a killer eagle on their doorstep, the sooner Grizelda and her master finish up this way the better."

What exactly was going on? Were the Russians charlatans, exploiting their birds? If the eagles were in such bad shape, how were they killing such quarry? Why was everyone so furious? Was it simply the prejudice that some establishment falconers, trainers of peregrines and gyrfalcons, have always borne against eagles? One of the aspects of golden eagle life that persistently escapes most casual birders is that they love to eat other birds of prey. If they have the

advantage of height they can outfly anything alive, even the legendary Arctic gyr. A nineteenth-century Persian, author of the trea-
tise *Baz Nama Y Nasiri* advises his pupils in ways to catch eagles so
that they might "hang them up and torture them." Saudi Arabian oil
sheiks, sponsors of many falconry events and exemplars of the most
hawk-mad culture on earth, ban all representations of eagles.

My friend John Loft, a scholarly British falconer of many years'
experience and wisdom, wrote to me with some observations. "A
good many falconers show an unreasonable prejudice against eagles.
It goes beyond the growls from those who say that they wouldn't take
the risk of flying such a dangerous creature, or complain that eagles
should never be flown when there are any other hawks in the field.
They really do get hostile, say that they shouldn't be flown at all. I
don't know what's behind it, but it may be jealousy."

Or, maybe, in a time when blood sports are packaged to seem
sanitary, harmless, even bloodless (see any modern book on fly fishing, with its Puritan emphasis on catch-and-release, if you doubt
this), chasing large animals with eagles puts onlookers too much in
mind of real hunger, of eating and its links with death. In such hunting, struggles and blood are inevitable, and, worse, visible. We like
our predation clean; our deaths off screen; our meat packaged. Or
at least some of us do. But, though I couldn't easily admit it to anybody, the more I heard, the more I wanted to see.

I SHOULD EXPLAIN AT THIS POINT THAT FOR ABOUT SEVEN
years I had no telephone in my rural New Mexican house. The only
way to contact me by phone was to call the local bar, the Golden
Spur Bar, a couple of dirt-road blocks away. I had a phone card and

could return a call by pay phone, if I had to. Since I have always been more comfortable making first contact by letter, this didn't bother me. I hadn't thought of its effect on someone who was uncomfortable writing in English. One day at four, as I stopped by the drive-by window to pick up my messages, the bartender handed me a yellow slip that said to call "Clara" at what seemed to be a Brooklyn exchange.

It took a few tries. My first call was answered by a male voice who with some difficulty managed to tell me that he did not speak English. He finally managed to say "Spell name." This took several minutes. He did use the name "Clara" a couple of times before he rang off, saying, "You call back." Then *she* left a message, which contained the words "eagle" and "Kazakhstan." When I called again, all the floodgates broke. Clara was voluble and quite articulate. She wanted to wait until we met to give me concrete information (I think now because she was most comfortable with her quite competent English face-to-face), but she confirmed her connections to Kazakhstan and to the eagle film shown at the falconer's meet. I had already intended to be in New York City in a few weeks, to meet with various publishers about possible projects. We arranged to get in touch and to meet in Brighton Beach.

Brighton Beach Station is on the far ocean side of Brooklyn, at the furthest apex of the train's loop. When I descended from the elevated platform into the hot summer sun, kids on skateboards shot through the crowd, looking like skate punks anywhere, shouting happy insults at each other in Russian. The crowd itself was a New York mix—Slavic-looking grandmothers wearing head scarves, Hispanics, young moms in shorts and athletic shoes pushing strollers, a few blacks—but Russian seemed to dominate the linguistic mix.

I looked around. Clara had said that she would send Yuri to pick me up. I was not expecting the golden-bearded, long-haired athletic man in his thirties in a bright yellow shirt and shorts, who moved toward me, smiling. He looked like a model for an adventure travel brochure, or a Patagonia ad. But he grinned, hooked a thumb back at himself in confirmation, and said, "Yuri." He then looked serious for a moment, as though struggling for the exact word, and motioned toward a high-rise apartment building on the beach side of the road. "This way," was what he finally came up with. "Clara."

The elevator rose eleven floors, beeping at each. A door popped open and Clara stood beckoning us in, a vivid presence. She was taller than I, wearing heels, a dress, heavy silver jewelry, rings, a lot of big hair. "Do you drink?" It was eleven A.M. I mumbled something noncommittal. "We have beer, wine—I do not drink. I am Russian. I just drink vodka." Somehow a bottle of beer appeared in my hand, and an enormous tray of salty delicacies appeared in front of us on a lacquered table. Permission was granted by all to smoke, anti-smokers be damned, and a lit cigarette handed to me despite my semi-sincere protests. "First," announced Clara, "we will see the film."

It was nothing less than amazing, despite its confusing (and semi-audible) narration. A quick view of a flying eagle against a mountainous background cut to two fox-hatted Kazakhs on horses, who dismounted to erect a long vertical net like one used for volleyball. They placed a tethered pigeon at its foot and rode off. I recognized what was going on; their rig was similar to a common hawk-netting setup, the *dho gazza,* but larger. Sure enough, in a few moments an eagle launched from a cliff and powered into and almost through the net.

The next sequences were familiar to any falconer; taming or "manning"; hooding and unhooding; stepping the bird on and off the glove; calling the still-tethered bird to a lure on a string—a fox skin garnished with "tidbits," of course. Only the fox-fur hats and the lattice walls of the ger's interior, hung with skins of lynx and fox, seemed exotic. One detail was fascinating. The newly-trapped eagle was perched on a thick swinging hammock of rope, so that she had to clutch and balance every time she moved. I had heard of this ancient technique for tiring and disorienting a wild bird, but had never seen it.

The hunt sequences were more unusual. The first and best featured a big tan fox. First, stirring music, black silhouettes of horsemen and their eagles against a bloody dawn. Then, landscape—vast, snowy, endless hills not unlike eastern Montana. A change in the music; a fox appears, out at the edge of vision, running. Cut to the eagle, still on her servant's fist. I could see her suddenly catch sight of something, tense, lower her head; signs any falconer could read. She leaps from his glove. Cut to the eagle, in the sky; cut to fox, running all out; cut to the rider, galloping forward; then to the eagle again. She begins to "stoop," to fall vertically, becoming an inverted, heart-shaped, head-down silhouette, pulls out for a moment, then falls again. Then the fox again, close in, who turns toward the camera as a black shadow enters the frame and covers him. A moment's flurry and the eagle's head comes up from her mantling wings. The body of the fox stirs once and is still.

The other sequences were fascinating but more ambiguous. The wolf was the most dubious, both cinematically rough and a bit unconvincing. The wolf appeared to be eating when the movie started and had worn fur around its neck. Was it baited in, which might have been fair; or a captive, which wouldn't? The wolf and the eagle only appeared together at the end (she *was* chasing it quite seriously) and there was a moment's break in the film at the kill, though she seemed to master it—if "master" is the right verb for a female eagle—after a moment.

The bird missed her strike on the deer, which was quite natural; many birds flying at swift ground quarry will fly into the ground if the quarry dodges, then be unable to regain enough speed to catch up again. But the lynx was the strangest battle of all. The lynx, which looked more like a huge American bobcat than a Canada lynx, was a fat healthy animal, much better looking than the wolf, though I did wonder what it was doing abroad by day. The eagle caught up to it in a woodland clearing and grabbed it with the rib-cracking grip that would have instantly disabled a canid but which didn't reckon with the lynx's four ripping, saber-tipped paws. The ensuing battle turned the snow pink and only ended when the Kazakh hunter came in and (discreetly, on the off-camera side) administered the coup de grace with his knife. I wasn't sure that I would ever fly a bird on such quarry, even if I coveted the skin.

Yuri accompanied the films with a constant chorus, each time the eagle appeared, of "Golden eagle, Aquila chrysaetos, *BERKUT!*" When they were done, Clara handed me another beer and asked if I would look at a few more unfinished strips. I sat through sequences of a child speaking in Kazakh to a crouching snow leopard; of flamingos flying above miles of shallow salt lakes in the sunset; of the agonizing, endless birth of a saiga antelope. They concluded their program with a high-spirited movie of hunting with *tazis,* elegant Saluki-like running hounds. When the last image faded, I applauded. I was dazed by alcohol and overwhelmed by the visuals. I knew, more than ever before, that I had to go there.

We—or, rather, Clara and I—exchanged bits of autobiography as Yuri tried to follow, smiling and frowning and occasionally interjecting quick sentences in Russian. Clara was not actually Russian; she was Hungarian but had been brought up partly in Russia. She had done well as an entrepreneur and had become some kind of a—self-defined?—trade representative. Yuri was a geography teacher, ethnically Russian, born in Kazakhstan.

Clara had met him there, after the fall of the Soviet Union. Yuri was a bone-deep romantic who probably would have been a back-to-the-land hippie in the US. His fascination with Kazakh culture and craft was not unlike that of some white Americans who become obsessed with Native American culture and art. Kazakhstan was in desperate economic straits, divided by Kazakh-ethnic Russian rifts. Yuri, with a foot in both camps, had persuaded Clara, with her contacts and money, to make several films on Kazakh hunting, nature, and culture. The eagle project was the most advanced, the most finished. But they needed a translation better than the one they had and were puzzled by the Americans' lack of interest.

Their translation was a problem. I had gotten some idea of this as they handed me a postcard by "Otan," the Kazakh conservation association, and a flier for the movie. The postcard was the mildest. It read "Otan (motherland) Kazakh nature conservation & "Kazmetalbank" are revived ancient kind of hunting-birds (golden eagle, falcon, hawk) and ancient race of Kazakh borzoi-tazy for badger, hare, fox, wolf, partridge, pheasant, and quail." It did help if you knew that a "Kazakh borzoi-tazy" was a dog, and the caption appeared to have little immediate relation to the photo, which showed three Moslem Kazakhs in colorful traditional dress, with an onion-domed Russian Orthodox church in the background. Still, it was possible to figure out.

The flier was a different matter. If I hadn't seen the films, it would have been totally incomprehensible; as it was, it was as unintentionally hilarious as a Japanese appliance manual. Across from a vivid painting of a stooping eagle with a horseman in the background, it proclaimed:

"The KAZAKH
ecological association
of keeping nature
OTAN

(Motherland)
PERFORMES
the only in the world film
about hunting with the golden eaglen
(Burkutshi)"

It went on to describe the eagle film (". . . catching of a golden eagle, upbringing, teaching the first catching animal") as well as "the musical nature "TRIPTIKH"—"Meeting," "Ballet of Love," "Borning"—meeting in the mountains with snow tiger, pink phlamingo, non-simple appearing to the world of saigak. (Sufferings of borning . . . on the phone of liric melody of the classic musik."

It's too easy to make fun of the considerable lengths that two idealistic non-English speakers had gone to in order to present their beloved Kazakhstan to an uncaring public, when I couldn't speak even one of their languages. Still, after several beers, I had to struggle to keep a straight face at some of the phrases. They showed me a narrator's script for the eagle film, which was full of good detail and incident once I got past the amazing title: "The Wingy." It covered the difficult course of training ("It's not a rare occasion that we come back from hunting with empty hands . . . without taking account of inevitable spots of shit, of course . . .") and, once in a while, digressed into the surreal, such as an account of Yuri's difficulties at the Brazil Eco Fest, when he was taken in by police and interrogated for "putting a cap on a sick parrot." I agreed to help them with a better narrative.

Their bigger problem, unyielding to any easy fix, was that the film was too realistic and too bloody for an America whose violence was only exceeded by its sentimentality. If falconers recoiled from some of its images, what could we expect from a media culture where self-appointed censors from both ends of the political spectrum were clamoring to excise all images that didn't fit their ideas of what was proper from the page and the screen? An editor from a national magazine, an older gentleman whose career predated these new norms, wanted some time later to run a Kazakh hunting piece, but was overruled by his board. He told me: "Apparently it's okay for eagles to hunt. But it's not okay for people to enjoy it."

A lesser problem was purely practical: despite their touching faith in me, authorship of a few obscure books didn't give me access to either free money or the airwaves. Still, I was inspired by the film. Doubts floated away on a flood of booze and camaraderie. Finally, I excused myself, doubting my ability to get back to midtown Manhattan if I had another drink or saw another movie. Yuri accompanied me to the subway. On the way down I noticed the beeping elevator again. I pointed to the speaker and imitated the sound: "Meeep!"

Yuri shook his head and sighed. "Beep, beep, beep, beep. Three focking years. *Not Kazakhstan.*"

A month later the Russians vanished without a trace. Clara called the bar once, when I wasn't there, but repeated phone calls rang into emptiness, and my letters were returned. They had left me an interesting clue, though. The *real* eagle masters, they had told me, were in the mountainous Kazakh province of Bayaañ Olgii, in western Mongolia, where Stalin had been unable to smash their traditions, and where grandfathers still passed on their wisdom.

It made sense. There, beyond the reach of Stalinist Russia and captive Kazakhstan, the Kazakhs, Turkic speaking "Free Warriors," had fled to the Altai mountains across the Mongolian border. They and their brethren once had conquered the area from the Altai to the Black Sea, then washed back and forth through Central Asia, riding with their cousins the Mongols under Chingiz, splitting from their oasis-dwelling kin, the Uzbeks, in the fifteenth century, then more recently from their fellow nomads, the Kirghiz. Disregarding boundaries, fleeing city-states ancient and modern, they had fetched up again in their ancestral mountains, where their legends tell that they were born of a mating of a man with a she-wolf. Later, David Edwards was to tell me about one octogenarian "grandfather" who still used the rifle with which he had killed the Russians who tried to stop him at the border in the thirties.

"THE GRANDFATHERS."—PATRICK'S CONCEPT. HE HAD SEEN the movies. "There's this scene after the hunt, right? There's all these guys with wolfskin hats and long mustaches, horses, big dogs, naked kids—this *inferno* blazing in the background. Right in front, this big female golden, unhooded, with all the kids running around. Then all of the sudden you get this old guy's face, all lit from the fire. He's talking, and the translator's sayin', 'The government took our birds, and now they give them back.' Then all of a sudden they're on to rug weaving, and I'm like, wait a minute, *wait a minute!* I mean, I just want to know one thing: *How do you teach them not to eat your kids?"*

He'd go on: "I think what they're showing now is bullshit. What did their GRANDFATHERS tell them? No scales to weigh the birds . . . no refrigeration . . . they must have had a level of consciousness we don't have, that we've lost . . ." And on, and on.

I was a bit more skeptical. Could they, as their detractors allege, just be cruder, more brutal, more callous than Westerners? But even as I said these things to myself, I know I didn't, couldn't, believe them. The search had taken on its own momentum, and I needed to get into that scene, make it more than a mere "picture."

HOW WOULD *YOU* GET TO MONGOLIA?

Recently, an interviewer asked me the intelligent question: "What does writing let you do that you couldn't do otherwise?" I answered, quickly, that it let me live the life I loved and to do odd things—falconry, travel, animal keeping. And, I added, "sometimes get paid for them."

As I said, quickly. While true, the answer, for me and many writers, is a gross oversimplification. At that time I was living at least half the year in the best place in the US for Central Asian contacts, Bozeman, Montana. What was once a sleepy little college town, where the National Collegiate Rodeo Finals were held once a year, had become a small city with perhaps the world's highest concentration of adventure travelers, fly fisher-persons, and extreme sportsters, not to mention unnatural concentrations of lawyers, MDs, and upland bird hunters with beeper collars on their dogs. It boasted of a food co-op, three fly-fishing stores, two bicycle shops, and the headquarters of more environmental organizations than, I believe, anything west of New York City.

Libby—then my wife-to-be—came back there ten years or so ago to run the mail-order section of an outdoor clothing business, when the town, to quote the owner of a local feed store, "used to be in Montana." As a former climber, Outward Bound instructor, and old Himalaya hand, her contacts seemed to include every American who had ever climbed in Asia, among them a friend from her high school days, Kent Madin, who was already running expeditions into western Tibet. I figured that Kent could point me in the right direction. Meanwhile, I needed both money and a plausible destination point.

If you ask the typical modern magazine writer how he gets to the Third World he will doubtless tell you that he makes a proposal to a magazine and they send him. But twenty-odd years of self-directed writing and five books in print have never connected me to *anything*. I did know a couple of good editors. One, at *Smithsonian*, was delighted by my proposal, until his board shot it down; he was the one that stated that it was okay for eagles to hunt, but not for humans to enjoy the spectacle. I sent a few more lines out, to editors who shall remain anonymous, but nobody bit. I got a color Xerox in the mail, of the eagle on the fox from the Russian movie. It was accompanied by a Xeroxed page in "Wingy" English, announcing a tour of the US by Yuri. It contained no return address, phone number, or e-mail address.

Since Kent hadn't yet seen an eagle in Asia, Libby called on an old friend from her Nepal days, who now ran an ecotour agency. He put me in touch with an Indian trek operator, who told me he could probably show me (molting, non-flying, summer) eagles in Kazakhstan for only $8,000, approximately half my income that year.

Then, a serious editor actually called. Terry McDonell, a restless spirit who had run everything from *Esquire* to *New York Newsday*, not to mention founding his own magazine and writing a novel, had suddenly been hired at the unlikely venue of *Sports Afield,* one of New York's three traditional hook-and-bullet magazines. I sent him a list of proposals, one of which was that he should stake me to a trip to Mongolia in search of the eagle people.

His reply was that he'd love to, but at present it was too exotic a subject. General sporting magazines, scrabbling madly for dollars in a declining market, had become tools of market research, which again and again told editors to give readers more of what they already had. But he did give me one hope. "If I ever get a real budget, I'll send you." I believed him, but the Kazakhs still seemed very far away.

Meanwhile, Western culture's appetite for the semi-wild and the exotic could not be denied; any place that became even marginally safe would soon draw the attention of ecotourists, even as those who wanted or needed to make their livings outside of the usual bounds found creative ways to take them there. Add to this mix the economic needs of those who lived under the bankrupt Soviet empire, and many bridges were soon started, though the first ones seemed to fall into the river. A "Montana-Kazakhstan Alliance" surfaced in the Montana papers; Libby went to its first workshop, where she met a Kazakh woman who seemed enthusiastic, and had a fax number in Almaty. Like Clara's address, though, it swallowed messages like a black hole, never emitting a single gleam of illumination.

Kent began to guide small groups to Mongolia, and other friends were pioneering new summer routes. Matt Wells, from Hailey, Idaho, and David Edwards, a photographer from Flagstaff, took a party to rivers in far northwestern Mongolia. I spoke to Edwards before he left, and asked him to keep his ears open for news of eagles. He had done a wonderful photo essay on the near-mythical Tsataan people, who live in teepees and ride reindeer, and I knew that eagle falconry would catch his eye. He was already mad about Mongolia, which he described as "Montana in the seventeenth century."

The smallest increments of contact encouraged me; they had to. In August Kent, just returned from his last trek, flagged me down as I browsed through the garlic at the Saturday farmers' market, to show me a photo of him with an eagle on his fist, taken just two weeks previously. Somehow, it validated the contemporary existence of the eaglers better than anything else so far. I went home walking on air, but the euphoria faded over the next few weeks as it always did when nothing else came up. Even a handsome postcard of Chingiz Khan from David Edwards failed to cheer me. It should have; all clues, ideally, should be met with delight and detachment, rather than euphoria or, worse, disdain and despair. The simple phrase—"I have a lead on some eagles etc."—was the pointer to my break, three years down the line: the beginning of the trail that would lead to Bayaan Olgii.

The next Mongolian contact was almost ridiculous: my stepson, Jackson, was invited to participate on a scouting expedition with Kent and David. I tried not to be envious; I would have killed for such an opportunity at seventeen, or forty-six. He helped carry vodka, rifles, a stun gun, and a computer as gifts for the Mongols; had an adventure, which he may tell elsewhere; rode, rafted, sang folksongs, fell off horses, learned a bit of Mongolian, observed, drank some vodka and fermented mare's milk, ate boiled sheep and grilled marmot; coined the phrase "marmot paraphernalia"; made friends, published—and was paid for—a mini-epic poem, and, frustratingly for me, saw not a single eagle.

A year passed. Another. Friends with more money than I went to Mongolia, again and again. I lost touch with Edwards for six months at a time; rumor would have it that he was adrift there, somewhere in that sea of grass and rock and sand. Editors and agents and publishers continued their silence.

THE HISTORY OF CENTRAL ASIAN BIRD-TRAINING PREDATES any pictures, never mind photographs, and makes a diverting study for the frustrated adventurer. The oldest reference I can find is in Marco Polo's memoirs, written a little more than seven hundred years ago, in 1293. His descriptions of Kublai Khan's hawking party read like something out of a fantasy novel (as some of his contemporaries seem to have believed it was). "He is accompanied by fully 10,000 falconers and takes with him fully 5,000 gerfalcons and peregrine falcons and sakers in great abundance, besides a quantity of goshawks for hawking along riversides . . . He always rides on the back of four elephants, in a very handsome shelter of wood, covered inside with cloth of beaten gold and outside with lion skins (a mode of conveyance which is rendered necessary to him during his hunting excursions, in consequence of the gout, with which he is troubled). Here he always keeps twelve gerfalcons of the best he possesses and is attended by several barons to keep him company. When he is traveling in this shelter on the elephants, and other barons who are riding in his train call out 'Sire, there are cranes passing,' and he orders the roof of the shelter to be thrown open and so sees the cranes, he bids his attendants fetch such gerfalcons take the cranes in full view while the Great Khan remains all the while on his couch. And this affords him great sport and recreation."

The great contemporary Russian wildlife artist, naturalist, and falconer Vadim Gorbatov has attempted to bring this nearly unbelievable scene to life, researching it meticulously through years of travel in Central Asia. A print hangs on my wall. The plains resemble eastern Montana, with a storm striding through the middle background like a malevolent living thing. The sky is alive with ducks, kites, and cranes. But you can almost *hear* the party, a churning mass of hunters, horses, falconers, and servants. Two gyrs climb toward the cranes, while another recovers from a strike. Sturdy little Mongol horses gallop past a tall golden Akhal-Teke from Turkmenistan. A cart of cheetahs is attended by Indians; Mongols and Tartars toss or restrain peregrines and goshawks. Tazi dogs lope through the crowd, or bend to bite thorns from their feet.

In the foreground rides a fat Kazakh, hooded eagle on his right arm, deer slung behind his saddle. The eagle only rates a passing mention from Polo, as though they are too mundane to dwell upon: "He has also a great many eagles trained to take wolves and foxes and fallow deer and roe deer, and these too bring in game in plenty." But Gorbatov, who has seen the Kazakhs hunt, places the simple country eagler front and center, just below the Great Khan's elephants.

Between Polo's time and the mid-nineteenth century the Kazakhs and Kirghiz must have continued to hunt with birds, even as they do today. The Central Asian cultures sometimes seem to stand outside history, raiding along its margins. The next reference in English I can find (which is possibly the next reference in print, period, predating the next in any language of falconry's bibliographer, J. E. Harting) is in Thomas Witlam Atkinson's *Oriental and Western Siberia: A Narrative of Seven Years' Explorations and Adventures in Siberia, Mongolia, the Kirghiz Steppes, Chinese Tartary, and Part of Central Asia,* published in 1859 in Philadelphia. His narrative of hunting deer with a "bearcoote" could stand today, if we admit that "he" was likely a female, and the "shackles" were leather cuffs rather than iron chains: "We had not gone far when several large deer rushed past a jutting point of the reeds, and bounded over the plain about three hundred yards from us. In an instant the bearcoote was unhooded and his shackles removed, when he sprung from his perch and soared up into the air. I watched him ascend as he wheeled round and was under the impression that he had not seen the animals; but in this I was mistaken. He had now risen to a considerable height, and seemed to poise himself for about a minute. After this he gave two or three flaps with his wings, and swooped off in a straight line toward his prey. I could not perceive that his wings moved, but he went at a fearful speed. There was a shout, and away went his keepers at full gallop, followed by many others. When we were about two hundred yards off the bearcoote struck his prey. The deer gave a bound forward and fell. The bearcoote had struck one talon into his neck, the other into his back, and with his beak was tearing out the animal's liver. The Khirghis sprung from his horse, slipped a hood over the eagle's head and the shackles upon his legs, and removed him from his prey without difficulty."

He adds: "Foxes are hunted in this way, and many are killed. . . The bearcoote is unerring in his flight; unless the animal can escape into holes in the rocks, as the fox does sometimes, death is his certain doom."

I continued to search through the old books. Between bursts of activity I would read and dream for hours, days, weeks; drinking, smoking, taking notes, combing book catalogs and footnotes for possible volumes that might mention the Kazakhs, the Kirghiz, Mongols and Mongolia. If a book had any possible reference to Central Asia I'd search its index for "Eagle" and "Falconry"; I sometimes threw books without indexes to the floor.

Old childhood favorites sometimes helped, but were as often hopeless. Roy Chapman Andrews, with his bullwhip and fedora, had introduced me to dinosaurs and ancient mammals in the halls of the Ames Free Library, and his adventures in the Gobi Desert were as much of an inspiration in their way as Kipling's animals. But he could be almost comically premodern, railing against "Chinamen," complaining that Chinese-Mongol "hybrids" have developed "an unfavorable combination of the worst characteristics of both races," referring to his servants as "boys." (He once justified his killing of whales by saying that they were sexually promiscuous.) His sole reference to eagles in *Across Mongolian Plains* (still a book worth reading) was to say that the "huge, golden eagles and enormous ravens made tempting targets on the telegraph poles."

A different kind of scholar provided more illumination. Both Andrews and Owen Lattimore came from what might be called establishment backgrounds. But while Andrews was a cheerful, unreflective colonial, Lattimore, born in China, was an independent-minded scholar-adventurer with no academic degrees, who would be attacked by Joseph McCarthy as "one of the top Communist agents in the country." A clipping hidden in my first edition of his *High Tartary* bears the headline "White House Aide, Lattimore Are Linked With the Reds." The text is a classic of the time's guilt by association; in it, not only does Lattimore deny that he is a communist and deny that he thought that Russia "should be allowed to take over Korea," but his colleagues, including an anti-communist witness, deny it as well. His crime seems to be that he "followed the techniques of secret Communists in some of his writings." In fact, the body of the piece seems to deny the headline.

Although his sympathy for peasants and the poor might have placed him on the left, Lattimore's travel writings never followed the party line. He and his wife aided refugees from communism. He was once refused a Soviet visa, and he said he was glad to have failed an examination for an Oxford scholarship because he thus escaped being "enamored of the extremist ideologies of the day." In his old age, a respected authority on Mongolia, he remarked that "the trouble with the New Left is that they haven't met a payroll."

But Lattimore was a lot more than a political controversialist; he was the first American scholar to enjoy the nomadic life lived by the Mongols and Kazakhs, and to share that life not only for many months in the thirties but intermittently for the next forty years. When I first read him on berkuts, I was amazed at his sensible intelligence, so different from the sensationalism of most accounts. "Like the hound, the *berkut,* the great hunting eagle of the Qazaqs, is used above all for taking foxes . . . the Qazaqs, however, everywhere maintain that the best of the eagles will take even a wolf unaided. . . Hares are of little value to the Qazaqs except for the skins, which are sold. Everywhere in Central Asia the hare, though sometimes eaten by the nomads, is not considered good clean food, but a wild relation of the cat."

Many of his odd observations would later prove to be true, even when they seemed unlikely. His knowledge of birds began to make even more sense to me a few years later, when I read the introduction to a new edition of his book *The Desert Road to Turkestan,* in which his son explained that, as a student in Tianjin, "he took up falconry and rabbit coursing with his Gansu greyhounds, Lanta and Lilith." Orville Schell, a writer of impeccable establishment academic background, wrote of him that he was "sensitive to the fact that he had never gone to college—much less graduate school, and called his happy boast—"My knowledge of China and Mongolia and Central Asia was not built up by having pull with the right people, but by traveling in the far interior, by studying Chinese and Mongol until I could read and speak and be completely independent"—"defensive." On the contrary, I found his attitudes irresistible, whether packing a box of two hundred spare monocles into the Gobi, serving food in Maryland in his Mongolian robes, reminiscing in his 1975 introduction to his late wife's *Turkestan Reunion* about his returning to camp "coming down from the forested slopes of a mountain having shot a roebuck or something else good to eat," only to self-deprecatingly add "proper male chauvinist pig stuff"; or in their "forty-four-year honeymoon" itself. But, even as he got me closer in imagination, I became more frustrated in reality. I had been reading, sitting, and dreaming too long.

AN ODD SEQUENCE BEGAN OUT OF THE BLUE. A FRIEND, THE range biologist Karl Hess, had been contacted by the government of Zimbabwe to bring out six journalists to see how their conservation system actually worked. They hoped to influence members of a United Nations conference to allow them to sell their harvested ivory. He immediately thought of me, and called to tell me I had three days notice before I would fly to Zimbabwe. How could I resist? I knew that I should be prepared for various tropical diseases, but how? Karl advised me that it would be winter there, with night time temperatures in the low forties. Since anti-malarial drugs take some time to be effective, I decided to just ignore them.

I spent ten days alternately dazed and delighted as we raced from one end of the country to another in cars and small prop planes. I saw my first elephant breaking down a tree over the dirt single-track road we were (illegally) taking as a shortcut to Hwange National Park, an hour before dusk. He seemed to be willing to dispute the right of way with our driver, and a little Japanese car seemed no match for his bulk, but he turned away at the last moment and we edged around the downed branches, trying not to think of what would happen if we got stuck. Mrs. Muza, our government guide, had already told us that a "European" had been eaten near Hwange a few years ago when he left his car at dusk.

We saw marvels, at an exhausting rate: lions, gray in our head-lights as we waited for the camp gates to open; a tower of circling vultures over the skeleton of a Cape buffalo, already picked clean; a seventeen-foot man-eating crocodile now confined as breeding stock at a state crocodile farm; more elephants, browsing on an acid-green lawn of new grass in the muddy margins of Lake Kariba. We watched the sun go down on the Zambezi River from a launch, while hippos and otters dived and surfaced in the liquid blaze of gold on the water, and giraffes ambled through the trees on the bank.

We also saw the remarkable success of Zimbabwe's innovative conservation programs, such as the CAMPFIRE (Communal Areas Management Programme for Indigenous Resources) system that returned money from the sustainable sale of wildlife products, and hunting permits, directly to the villages in the area. We saw the damage that a population explosion of elephants could do, in the form of giant baobab trees ripped to shreds like tissue paper. We heard testimony from villagers who once hated and feared elephants and now appreciated them. We saw a game farm run by an irascible old Afrikaaner with muttonchop whiskers and a handlebar mustache who insisted on calling me "Greenpeace"; and, the next day, heard him defended as a hero by the black head ranger of the nearby park. We also saw a darker side to wildlife preservation, in the statement by another black ranger about why he was successful: "I kill more poachers!"

The mix of exotic sights, sounds, and smells, the frenetic pace, the amount of information we had to digest; the attempt to come to terms with, not two, but several cultures trying to live with each other, all contributed to a kind of sensory overload. On our last stop we stayed at a new lodge on Lake Kariba. I remember sitting on a porch overlooking the lake, watching a pied kingfisher rattle past a white-headed fish eagle, drinking a gin-and-tonic, and saying "this has enough quinine in it that I won't *ever* get malaria." Everyone laughed.

That night we found that a reservation screw-up had left two of us, my old friend Tom Wolf and I, with a single bed under a shroud of mosquito netting. I elected to sleep on the porch; the weather, cool in the highlands, had turned stifling, and the early evening was bug free. I tossed restlessly all night; a lion was roaring less than a mile away, and a hyena paraded back and forth along the unnervingly low electric fence all night long, uttering the oddly innocent-sounding "eee-*rup?*" with which this dangerous predator queries the night. Toward dawn I heard the buzz of a mosquito or two, but I don't really remember a single bite.

Two weeks later, after I had returned from Zimbabwe, the realization hit me, as suddenly as the spasm of teeth-rattling shivering that had made it impossible for me to keep driving. We were headed out to Arizona from my New Mexico home to move my stepson from one college to another. But, despite the ninety-plus temperature outside, I felt colder than I ever have in my life.

"I've got malaria." Libby was initially skeptical, but after a quick check of the *Lonely Planet* guide to Zimbabwe, which I had brought along to continue the research that had taken me there, she had to agree. I didn't just feel sick; I felt stupid. For a writer to come down with malaria immediately after his first trip to Africa was ridiculous, a cliché. Or as a friend put it, "Isn't it . . . traditional?"

Like many tropical travelers, I didn't know much about malaria, or its treatment, and much of what I "knew" was wrong. First was the idea that malaria was confined to the tropics, rare around civilization. In fact, malaria is almost everywhere, and is returning to many places, like the southern US, where it had been "vanquished." It was once found in the Ohio River Valley and on Staten Island—and could return there. Even worse, the new strains tend to be drug-resistant.

The number of bad assumptions I made astonishes me now. The International Association for Medical Assistance to Travelers publishes up-to-date brochures on malaria distribution, prevention, and medicine, which among other things could have told me that the Zambezi River valley, where I was bitten, is year-round home to *falciparum,* the "malignant" drug-resistant malaria, and that even partial protection might have spared me. "Malignant?" Another of my assumptions was that malaria was unpleasant and annoying, but not deadly. Wrong again. *Falciparum* can kill even healthy first-time victims in days, and most strains resist chloroquine, the most common and least damaging drug used. If you are not properly diagnosed, you are in very deep trouble. There are four kinds of malaria, and the symptoms of all are similar; only a blood test can tell which type you have.

Medicines are still another can of worms. Traditionally, the quinine in the evening's gin-and-tonics worked as a preventative (and, oddly, quinine is making a comeback in certain areas were malarias have developed a resistance to chloroquine). But even there, the dosage goes beyond that likely to be ingested by the most devoted gin-drinker. Chloroquine still provides some protection, if not a cure. Lariam (mefloquine), the most effective cure, has a circus of ugly side effects, not the least of which is potential temporary psychosis.

It was a weekend, and we were in Arizona, so it took me two days to get to my doctor's office in New Mexico. During that period my temperature spiked up to 106 degrees, not once, but twice. I was wracked by chills that nearly threw me off the bed. Joint pains sought out every old break and arthritic hinge in my body. My headache was so bad that I couldn't bear any light. After the first almost simultaneous eruption of puke and liquid feces, I didn't seem to have anything left to flush, but the fat melted visibly off my bones. From the state of my drenched sheets, I suspect most of it left in sweat. I could neither sleep nor pass out. I was too delirious to remember much, but Libby told me later that I'd periodically sit up and declaim in a tone of wonder: "This is *extremely* interesting."

I dragged myself in as soon as the office opened, demanding drugs in a loud voice. Although I was almost too weak to stand, I was in the beginning of the twenty-four-hour respite that *falciparum* gives its victims before the fever returns. He laughed, took a blood sample, gave me a prescription for chloroquine, told me to come back if the symptoms did, and left for his month-long vacation in Ireland. I didn't get the report on my blood test until after he returned; the office staff didn't think it important for me to know which of the four malarias I had, despite *falciparum*'s potential deadliness and its re-sistance to chloroquine.

Now came my only stroke of luck. Karl Hess, the biologist who had arranged my trip to Africa, called to see how it went. When he heard my story he immediately drove up from Las Cruces, three hours away, to deliver me a two-pill dose of an anti-malarial called Fansidar, from South Africa. "Chloroquine doesn't work on Zambezi malaria." Now they tell me.

The Fansidar did its job: I slept for twelve hours, and the fever never came back. Still, in that short time, I had lost so much weight that I could barely recognize myself in the mirror; I hadn't weighed that little since I was twenty. I was also deeply anemic. When *falciparum* plasmodia are rampaging through the bloodstream, the tiny vampires can eat a quarter pound of hemoglobin in an hour. Two months later I could walk around the block, slowly. I can't recommend the disease as a weight-loss method.

The last malarial myth is that the symptoms will recur, again and again. The most serious, *falciparum,* doesn't. But, while the other three species are milder, primaquine, taken to prevent their recurrence, can cause severe anemia in individuals from ethnic groups lacking the G6PD enzyme, including many from Africa, Asia, the Middle East, and the Mediterranean. Lariam, while still the most effective current anti-malarial, does not limit its side effects to temporary psychosis; there have been a few fatal toxic reactions to the drug. The most promising new anti-malarial, not yet available in the US, is Artemisinin, derived from the traditional Chinese medicinal plant Quinghaosu. Chinese pharmacologists have found that it cures chloroquine-resistant *falciparum* in mice and humans, with far fewer side effects that Mefloquine. Clinical tests are starting in the US, although a friend, an Army veterinary pathologist, says that massive doses caused brain tumors in dogs!

MEANWHILE, BACK IN THE WORLD, TERRY MCDONELL HAD jumped to *Men's Journal*. I had become so fascinated by the subject of malaria that I pitched him an article on my near-death experience, which he bought. When he asked what else I might want to write about, I reminded him of the Kazakhs and their eagles. He commented that I was "deeply weird," but that he would think about it. It was August, 1997.

"Eagle season" runs from November through February. In December, a call from *Men's Journal* came in. Would I consider going to Mongolia *immediately?* It can take six weeks to get a visa; I plunged in. Despite my hatred of telephones and forms, they became my life. Matt Wells faxed equipment lists; Jackson modified them. Libby called her former employer for clothing. I was advised not to put "writer" on my Chinese visa application; I ended up listing myself as a "livestock breeder," true if dogs, pigeons, and falcons are livestock. *Men's Journal* wanted me to carry my own expenses, and be reimbursed on my return; I explained patiently that, had I enough money to go myself, I'd already be there. They agreed to pay up front for my ticket.

On February 13, 1998, I arrived at the Los Angeles airport with three stuffed bags. I was already over budget; a frantic last-minute fax from David, all the way from Bayaan Olgii in far western Mongolia, insisted that I bring three pairs of binoculars, three headlamps, six expensive knives, ten red head scarves, and more, as gifts. I had a tentative agreement from him to photograph, another agreement from Arizona filmmaker Ed George (sent by Terry to join me at the last minute) to help him with food and hotel costs, the assurance that a translator was waiting in Mongolia, and a few hundred dollars in my pocket. I was about to jump off the long-awaited cliff, and hoped that I could fly.

ED FOUND ME IN THE MCDONALD'S AT LAX, TWO HOURS after I arrived. He is a wiry, athletic, graying professional of about fifty, Californian in style, casual in manner. He never seems to worry about schedules or time; nevertheless, he always seems to make it to the gate. My formality and nervous punctiliousness—I wear sports jackets on planes, he takes his shoes off—can contrast oddly with his laid-back dress and attitudes. But we shared fascinations with fly fishing, wildlife, and food. As long as we avoided certain dangerous subjects, we were able to function well as a team. We checked through the list of gifts recommended by Dave Edwards and inventoried our reading matter, which we knew was important on backcountry trips (we both read, a more important common ground than you might think). Ed was also bringing more camera equipment than I suspected existed in western Mongolia, a truly amazing amount of high-tech baggage. We filled up on cheap American hamburgers for the last time, and headed out for the international gate.

The long flight from Los Angeles to Beijing was made longer by Eastern China Airline's cattle car ambiance, and weird food; our first meal consisted of Chinese noodles, a "salad" of potatoes, whole tomatoes, and mayonnaise, two slices of harshly chemical Chinese sausage, American cheese, a sweet bean paste pastry, tea, and beer. When I requested a soporific vodka, the waitress ignored me.

If the food was strange, the movies were odder: three Sino-Japanese martial arts epics dubbed into Chinese with English subtitles and a murky DeNiro Brooklyn epic with Chinese subtitles that would have been remaindered if it had been a book.

The view out the window was far more interesting, although my keeping my window shade open annoyed my fellow inmates. We flew in a curve following the edge of land up along the California coast, edging British Columbia, Alaska, the Aleutians and on across to Asia. After about Juneau the view was of tortured shapes in ice-white and blue, endless mountains, bays framed in glaciers, fields of snow, and frozen rock. This brutal but fearfully beautiful terrain would continue down the coast of the Asian landmass, through Kamchatka, almost to Beijing. I found it dazzling, dozing on and off, watching the electric dot of our progress on the video screen move as slowly as an hour hand. The landscape below seemed a precursor of where we were going.

Beijing at dusk was slightly ominous, at once alien and strangely familiar. The terminal was filled with the crushing crowds common to Third World airports, but more prosperous and purposeful. After rounding up our baggage a few queries pointed us toward the shuttle bus for our nearby one-night luxury hotel. Outside the air was chilly and smelled pleasantly of coal smoke. Chinese yuppies in business suits, talking in peremptory tones on cell phones, pushed through thick clots of baggage handlers with worn felt work clothes, scars, and snotty noses. Despite their coarser clothes, they seemed more cheerful than the businessmen. Although the sun was still up, it was invisible in the thick haze.

We had picked the hotel because it was "in" the airport, allowing us to leave without worry in the morning even with jet lag hangovers. Apparently, though, it was still more than a half hour away. The bus moved slowly through streets so different from one another they appeared to be on different continents—the US, LA perhaps, on one block; sub–Saharan Africa on another. Glass high rises with roofs too far above us to see from the bus windows, surrounded by walls and serviced by Mercedes, alternated with black alleys lit by low yellow lights that illuminated piles of vegetables, heaps of loose bricks, old cars swarming with enthusiastic mechanics, like the dimly lit poor streets of Harare—half Third World, half gated-enclave future. The squalor of the alleys seemed more humanly inviting to me than the cold, gleaming skyscrapers. After checking through an opulent lobby overrun with what seemed like hundreds of servile staff supervised by a stolid Swiss woman with plastic hair, I pried open the window of my room to cool, thick, smoky air and the intermittent reports of firecrackers. They would sound all night long; but for the ever-present "security" of walls and guards, you would think the peasants were still staging a revolution.

The murk began to pale after seven, to reveal the same strange Blade Runner world in a bit more clarity, its contrasts even more pronounced by the yellow-gray light of day. I am accustomed to sticking my head out the hotel window on my first day in any new country to see some totemic new bird. I rolled back the curtains and peered out expectantly but nothing flew. A vista of old rooftops and industrial blocks pierced by high rises faded into the dully luminous air, which in my imagination resembled that of Sherlock Holmes's London, circa 1880. Finally a single rather dirty common pigeon flew up to a roof. It didn't bode well for my life list.

A better omen, despite its own confinement, awaited us on the way to breakfast. Tethered in an ornamental courtyard on a six-foot rope, walled from the circular entrance drive by an ornamental facade, stood a gigantic pale Bactrian camel, blinking placidly, like an ambassador to the interior. We stuffed ourselves with a western-style buffet breakfast and herded our cart of luggage back onto the shuttle. By day, the streets, unlike the glossy international facades, were cheerfully alive, although the ground surrounding them was a beaten down mat of brown grass and iron-hard dirt. A flock of huge sheep grazed in the median, while groups of middle-aged men and women, some in ties and business suits, performed tai chi under carefully groomed trees. Bicyclists cut between limos with loads of groceries on their backs. The humans, if not the machines, seemed happy. Finally, in a grove of low trees that resembled a spindly orchard, I spied, first, a circular stick nest, and then not just one, but a flock of brilliant black-capped corvids with blue wings and long tails: Azure-winged magpies. As in my previous trips to Zimbabwe and Provence, a member of the crow family, most primate-like of birds, had come through.

PART 2

The Dream Made Real

Beijing, at least the part we touched, is a modern city-state, a placeless place. But when we boarded the plane for Ulaan Bataar, I suddenly felt we were entering Asia. Just ahead of us in line was a Moslem patriarch, a Kirghiz I think, with hawk features on carved walnut skin, a trimmed white beard, a long wool coat, a round *kepesh* cap. His white-scarved wife tucked the ends of her head covering around her face out of Islamic modesty, or maybe just against the cold.

Aloft, a familiar kind of country unfolded beneath me. Because I love maps, I love deserts and airplane windows. The country below us, while not yet desert, was big and dry and minutely carved by both humans and water. The desiccated, dissected country north of Beijing resembled the hills of New Mexico, with the startling addition of the serpentine Great Wall. Northward, the landscape progressed in bands as I pored greedily over it. First, snowy low mountains, still dry-looking and brown; next, terraced forms, which in turn gave way to a flatter, intricately herringboned kind of irrigated cropland. And on, inexorably, to a crinkled snowy desert that seemed suddenly unpopulated.

It was only the beginning of the great dry Asian interior. The crinkles smoothed out as though an enormous hand had flattened them with the edge of a board, and roads disappeared. The ground became incredibly flat, and I knew we were over the Gobi, the edge of the "real" Mongolia. And then we just flew, into a brown void, as though hypnotized. A moment of panic, not for the first or last time, flared into that void: what the *hell* did I think I was doing? I had no money to speak of, knew little Russian, no Chinese or Mongolian, never mind Kazakh; dubious contacts, a little outdated knowledge, insomnia, arthritis that made riding a horse or jeep for any length of time uncomfortable, and a companion who knew less about the whole deal than I did, and for whom I was responsible, even as he dozed in the seat beside me. And we were headed for mountains on the other side of *Mongolia,* on the far side of the Gobi Desert and enough roadless plains to fill up both Dakotas, Wyoming, and Montana put together. Had I lost my mind?

There was nothing to do but stare out the window into that eerily familiar void. Going out into the desert soothed me in New Mexico; now, somehow, the desert landscape did its work again. Wrinkles of hill top and rock ridge appeared again below us, holding skiffs of snow the way they did back home. Just before Ulaan Bataar the land began to rise up and crests of conifers poked through the deepening snow drifts, while odd round corrals appeared on the south sides of the hills, surrounded by sunbursts of radiating hoofprint trails. Wherever this country was, we were coming into it.

IT WAS DARK AGAIN. THE TERMINAL WAS YELLOW-LIT AND full of bodies, the tallest of which revealed itself to be David Edwards, more bearlike and grizzled than ever in layers of frayed Patagonia and a new mustache. He was roaring greetings, picking up bags, and starting stories before I could even open my mouth. Beside him stood a tall quiet figure in a belted leather coat and a leather cap with earflaps. "This is Canat. He'll be your guide and interpreter. I'd trust my life to him—he's *brilliant.* God, the things you're going to see—images out of *myth,* I tell you . . ."

As David roared on, I shook Canat's hand. He had a round dark face, black eyes, a warm smile with many very white teeth. He seemed incredibly young. On the phone David had spoken of his being a former Russian commando, *Spetsnaz,* then a veteran of Russian prisons, a one-time binge drinker and street fighter turned guide and entrepreneur. None of it showed in his unlined face.

David steered us through the airport so fast I have no recollection of customs, and into the back of a taxi with no door handles (we soon found this to be the common condition of Ulaan Bataar taxis, whether late-model Mercedes or the kind of aged Russian sedan that resembles a 1962 Chevy II Nova made out of plasticine by an untalented five-year-old.) The night was incredibly, oppressively freezing, dank, full of a now-familiar coal-fired mist, and blacker than the darkest backcountry American town. What few lights there were seemed dimmed to fogginess by the mist and smoke of the almost palpable air.

We drove down a long, straight, two-way street into what dimly resembled a blacked-out city. There were plenty of cars and constant movement, but there were no street lights, and the almost total absence of commercial lighting added to the gloom. Finally we arrived at a square with one postmodern cube, brightly lit—the BISHRELT: VERY GOOD HOTEL: NIGHTCLUB.

The Bishrelt was to become our home, on and off, for over a month, and again in a couple of visits two years later. But at that moment we gave it very little attention. We paused briefly at a desk manned by subteens, then climbed a curving flight of stairs, past remnants of construction that suggested the building had not always been a luxury hotel, to a high wooden door that led into a large, brightly lit, extremely hot room. The toilet was decorated with a paper strip that said in Cyrillic and English: "DISINFECTED FOR YOU."

David pulled off a couple of layers of clothing, popped a can of German beer, and attacked our packs. He pronounced our presents "splendid" and my little Leica "a professional's point-and-shoot." It was apparent that he had spent the past months seeing marvels, more than our fast trip would be likely to allow us, and that he was bursting to share them. "The Kazakhs are incredible, *incredible.* A fourteenth-century chronicle says that they prepare for war as though going to meet a bride . . . we sleep on wood floors, in cabins, you know. Did you bring earplugs? Sometimes it's too noisy . . . too close, too long, too loud . . . the kids, the animals . . . Don't drink *too* much vodka . . . it gets tiresome . . . it'll get to your gut. You should see them ride . . . they can ride horses straight up rock walls . . . they say they can ride to places they could never get to before when they're riding up to an eagle kill. You'll see things out of *legend.*"

He related to me for the first time a story I would hear again in Olgii, about an eagler who, a couple of months before, had his eagle killed by a snow leopard she was attacking. "He told me, 'I found myself crying.' He has it frozen in his cold house, waiting for spring, trying to decide what mountain to pick so he can bury her in the sky." He spoke of endless hospitality, of bottomless feasts of fat sheep and vodka, of falconry practices among old men that were too ancient to call medieval: giving birds crushed ice to lower their weight, sugar to increase their aggression, rabbit-skin mittens to warm their wings. I was open-mouthed; despite his constant reiterations of "you probably know this," I did not, *could* not. Canat leaned in the corner, at rest, a half-smile on his face, a stance that would become familiar.

Then David stood. "I've arranged for us to have dinner at an Indian restaurant with some people from here—some embassy people, UN attachés, and an old French photographer. You'll love him. We've got to be there in half an hour." He hustled us down the stairs again, past the kids watching TV in the lobby—one stood to open the door for us, as he always would—and into the savage cold of the outside, where our taxi was waiting for another drive into the inky streets.

The restaurant could only increase our sense of disorientation. Hazara, apparently the "in" place-of-the-moment for expats of every description, nationality, and gender, was built in the shell of some monstrous Soviet-era brick-shaped concrete warehouse. But its proprietor had come up with an elegant solution, filling the entire second floor with a flock of mythical mogul-style silk tents, subtly lit from within. Although the building retained a chill, inside the tents it was warm, golden, and scented with delicious smells.

The table already held a crowd: many French, a few Dutch, one German, an Englishman, and a couple of New Yorkers. The conversation paused ever-so-slightly to admit us and immediately resumed its babble. I thought immediately and with no kindness at all: *expatriates!*

The woman across from me, whose lips had that collagen-enhanced look, was pointed at me by David, who called me "our bird of prey expert." Apparently she had been told of Mongolia's endangered falcons by another New Yorker, who was busy yelling in the old Frenchman's ear. She wasn't particularly interested. She did want to know where I was from. When I told her New Mexico, she told me she knew it well, and loved its "spirituality." Where had she been? I queried. Taos and Santa Fe, said Ed slyly. She agreed, amazed.

The Dutch UN official asked how long we were staying. When I told him about a month, he launched into a tirade on the immorality of flying visits. I agreed, quoting Peter Beagle, who wrote my travel motto: "Wherever I go, I always want to spend a lifetime there. Anywhere—Tashkent, Calabria, East Cicero. I always want to be born there and grow up and be horribly ignorant and die. I don't approve of flying visits." I asked him if he knew where we could get funding to stay longer. He changed the subject.

The German asked me to take a photo of him and his boyfriend before they left for the disco. I obliged, and later it came out quite well. Unfortunately, I had lost his address by then.

On my right, David was dispensing advice in my and Ed's direction faster than we could ever take it down or remember it, while simultaneously sharing photographic data with the Frenchman. "They'll seat you at the head of the table. First, wash; or if water's short, move your hands over your head as though you're washing, and say 'Bismillah.' Then take your knife—right hand, *never* left— you can steady the sheep's head with the left—cut toward you, *never* away. Cut a piece off the lip and give it to the eldest son; then another and give it to your host. *Right* hand, boyo, remember. Then cut some good pieces, lots of fat . . ."

The old photographer, Roland, was also holding court on the Kazakhs. He was the lion of this gathering, and I must admit he was a charming old rogue: a dapper, almost stereotypical Parisian with a hawk's profile and a neat white beard, red wine in one hand, cigarette in the other. I have since seen one of his books of photography, on Afghanistan, and, though I prefer seeing things myself or reading books made of words rather than pictures, must admit it is excellent. He kept saying: "I am ze *French* Moslem."

THE OTHER NEW YORKER CAME DOWN THE TABLE AS I FINISHED my third beer, and accused me of being a falconer. I was, it seems, directly responsible for the coming extinction of all falcons. I was somehow linked to a recent incident at the Ulaan Bataar airport, where a US "Sikh" was discovered in possession of thirty or forty saker falcons, en route to the Arabian Gulf.

Now this was really interesting, if not in the way my inquisitor thought. "Endangerment" of falcons is a complicated issue. Probably no *species* of falcon has ever been endangered except the Mauritius kestrel, a robin-sized bird confined to a single South Pacific island. But several populations of the ubiquitous (literally—it is found on all continents and major islands except Antarctica, and gets pretty close to there) peregrine were indeed knocked to their knees by DDT metabolites in the years after World War II, especially in the eastern US and western Europe. This was logical enough—it was where industrial farming was most common.

It was also where our story-of-the-month obsessed media thrives. "Endangered peregrines" and stories about their reintroduction in cities (like New York) became, and still are, staples of the "news lite" sections of all our metropolitan papers. The "still are" is especially ironic because populations around the world have not only recovered but soared to pre-pesticide levels—and had done so by 1982, when scientist Tom Cade, the man most responsible for their reintroduction, declared them both unendangered and "recovered." They are in fact the greatest success of the Endangered Species Act, and have since then been celebrated for just that reason.

But the peregrine projects threw the spotlight on falcons, and especially their use in falconry by the oil sheiks. For all I knew the Sikh (a New Mexican) might indeed be the sleazy entrepreneur he stood accused of being. But his actions were unlikely to endanger the saker, whose breeding numbers were estimated by Tom Cade to be in the area of 100,000 *pairs,* none endangered by pesticides.

So I rose to the bait, asking my interrogator how many birds he thought the Arabs "consumed." He hadn't the slightest idea. I told him that the best estimate was that about three thousand birds were trapped and flown each year, and that virtually all Arab birds were then released. He said he assumed that, at that point, they died. I explained, with a bit of condescension, that they were used for hunting; Why would they die? When he said that they were too far from home, I realized that he didn't know that Central Asia falcons naturally migrated to the Middle East. When I explained *that,* he accused me of lying, of ignorance; that birds flew straight south. I gave up.

Exhausted and not a little depressed, I turned to Canat, who had been quietly eating on my left, taking in all the noise with no comment. He seemed to me to be the only self-contained person at the whole roaring table. I knew that he hoped to become a regular guide, that David had been his first client, and a few other maybe-facts. "Were you really Spetsnaz?" I blurted.

He winced a little. "No, just Russian soldier. I am small businessman. I want to get my English better, buy little hotel, show travelers my Kazakh country. We are very poor there." He went on talking of the beauty of that country, of snow leopards and eagles.

"Is hunting with eagles a living tradition? Or just something of the past? Is it just for show? I mean, are we really going to see eagles hunt?"

Canat looked at me, grinned broadly, and gave me the reply I came to know well. "Of *course!*"

MORNING COMES ON SLOWLY IN ULAAN BATAAR. MONGOLS are not a culture of early risers, at least not in winter. The square below the windows of the Bishrelt seems wrapped in a fog despite the city's semidesert situation. Single pedestrians wander through the pockmarked street, wrapped in scarves, heads covered with round fur hats. It looks like predawn down there, but in fact it is eight-thirty. The sun has not yet broken through, though whether it is behind the mountains or shrouded in coal smoke I cannot tell. I fog the window with my breath and watch for birds. Soon, a raven strokes past the imperial facade of the old Lenin museum across the street. I want to go exploring, but the city doesn't seem ready.

The day actually began, as it would many times, with a surreal breakfast in the Bishrelt's dining room. A smiling teenaged boy with a ponytail greeted us and bowed us in; we were the only guests eating breakfast. The waitress, also in her teens and wearing heel taps on her shoes, apparently a dress requirement for Bishrelt staff, came to take our order. Ed pointed to "omelet" on the menu, and I smiled and said "two." She brought us two cups of instant coffee, and turned on a boom box playing disco music in, I believe, Rumanian. It was extremely loud, echoing through the bare room.

Now began a ritual which would confound us as long as we ate at the Bishrelt. Still another teenager, this one male, tapped up to bring us each a slice of prewrapped American cheese (still in its wrapper), a hot dog, a piece of sliced white bread, a sealed container of jam, and a lump of fried dough. He bowed and said, "Bon appétit."

I stared. Ed opened his menu and again pointed to "omelet." The waiter bowed. Perhaps things would have proceeded a bit more smoothly at that point, but Ed decided to up the ante by asking for a "cheese" omelet. He picked up his slice of cheese food and mimed putting it into the nonexistent omelet. The waiter bowed again and returned to the kitchen, clicking as he went. I took a bite of the hot dog, apparently the "sausage" on the menu. I was famished, but it was the second-worst member of the sausage family I ever ate (the worst was in London) with an amazing metallic taste.

I envied Ed until his waiter returned with the omelet: a pancake-sized disk of dried egg, with four perfect pats of melted cheese food spaced equidistantly around its edges in a perfect symmetry which reduced me to giggles. We decided with the cold outside that we'd best eat what we had (although Ed drew the line at the hot dog) and gagged it down while the waitress returned with more coffee, accompanied by an entire plate of sugar cubes.

Let me enter here a partial roster of Bishrelt breakfasts that we compiled weeks later as we waited for our plane, given in the order that we ate them.

1. I order an omelet: get fried dough.
2. I order an omelet, and Ed orders a boiled egg by drawing it on his napkin. We both get omelets.
3. Ed orders a "cheese omelet" and gets one.
4. Ed orders a boiled egg by finding and pointing at the eggshells under the counter; gets it.

5. We order an omelet and a boiled egg, and each get two hot dogs and a ball of fried dough.
6. We order tea and coffee and get two coffees.
7. We order tea and coffee and get two teas.
8. We order tea, coffee, and two omelets and get what we ordered.

Every order comes with individually wrapped cheese food slices.

Lunch and dinner, though sometimes similarly afflicted by randomness, could be delicious once you realized that anything with fish or vegetables belonged in the realm of myth. I became so fond of one dish, called "garlic soup with" on the menu, that the bon appétit waiter would bring me a huge bowl every evening, with a shot of Genghis Khan vodka and a German beer, before I ordered the entree. This seemed to be exactly what was described: a rich, garlicky meat broth with whatever leftover meat was available. Entrées included "fillet of beer," stewed potota," "Ox tunque snack," and "chicken FANTASY," all of which were delicious except for the fantasy, which apparently didn't exist.

LEAVING THE HOTEL BROUGHT US FROM THE LOW-COMEDY venues of fancy Third World hotels into a place that was completely foreign, as quickly as the closing of the door behind us. The cold was startling, profound. I have lived in Montana in the winter and hunted on its eastern plains; this was different. Perhaps the landscape of vast open man-made spaces and pavement lent their own chill to the air; perhaps it was actually colder, for thermometers would remain rare throughout our stay. I know I instantly wished, despite the brilliant sun now revealing itself over the Soviet-style apartment blocks and the utter lack of wind, that I had worn a hat that morning.

The city was bright and dry and finally, after ten A.M., bustling. A red Russian Jeep idled at the corner, its hood covered with a shaggy calfskin complete with legs. We headed toward the outskirts of town, where we hoped to see Buddhist temples and suburbs of what we soon found out were *not* to be referred to as yurts, through enormous squares, populated by throngs of pedestrians—from *haut chic* Mongolian women in leather and fur, to nomads with felt boots and long belted robes, the traditional *deel*.

Beyond the squared-off skyline of rectangular rooftops soared blue and white mountains that would not be out of place in Big Sky. Two huge stacks, like the nuclear coolers at Three Mile Island or the ones in *The Simpsons,* spewed damp smoke into the brilliant air; we would learn that they provided the steam heat that kept all municipal interiors warmed to at least seventy-five degrees Fahrenheit, making the cold outside seem even harsher. Ravens soared overhead, harassed by smaller crows with a local accent: *carr.*

The streets were a festival of culture collisions. A red-robed Buddhist priest with an earflapped cap and boots with turned-up toes cut between two Mercedes sedans at a traffic stop. An ad proclaimed "St Valentins Day" in English and Cyrillic characters. Sleek Japanese-made cars, looking like police cars anywhere, proclaimed "POLICE", in English only, on their sides. A bearded man rode along the sidewalk on a pony, past a drunk pissing into an iron-hard snow bank decorated with used condoms. People here were obviously hardy. Unlike in Beijing, everybody seemed to be smiling; women grinned right into your face. It occurred to me that in twenty years this could be an international fun sports capital like Bozeman or Sun Valley. The thought depressed me; it might make everyone richer, and they deserved it, but I knew I'd definitely prefer this cheerful subarctic squalor.

We wandered through the open squares like the tourists we had temporarily become, possessed by curiosity and impatience. This was Mongolia proper, as exotic as Mars, but not where we wanted to be. We wouldn't even know when we could fly to Bayaan Olgii, the capitol of the Kazakhs, until we visited the airline offices later in the day with David and Canat. Meanwhile, it wasn't hard to marvel.

A great temple loomed hazily on the eastern horizon, visible above the rooftops. We crossed a final modern street and found ourselves in AD 1200 with TV antennae: a ger (the Mongolian word for "yurt"—the Mongolians do not like to use the Russian word) suburb of hundreds of round felt buildings, each surrounded by a wood-pole fence like the coyote fences of rural New Mexico. Flags and pennants fluttered above, while tufts of sheep hide stuck out of the frozen snow and mud under our boots. Ravens were everywhere, perched on the flags and fences, squabbling with dogs in the gutter, stroking across the dark-blue sky holding pieces of plastic in their beaks. So, except for the plastic, would it have been in the camps of the Plains Indians, or in Elizabethan London.

A short skinny man detached himself from a doorway and skittered up to us. He was a positively archetypal beggar: shaved head, filthy clothes, three visible teeth, and a snotty nose. "Want to buy Mongolian antique? Very old, very old!" He skipped along beside us.

"Isn't it illegal to take antiques out of the country?" I asked, misunderstanding his level of English. He ignored me.

"Very old, very old! Buddhist antique!" He unwrapped a filthy piece of cloth to disclose two beautiful objects: a stone snuff bottle of lapis lazuli, dotted with golden pyrite stars, and a tiny, intricately wrought silver spoon. I looked at Ed and saw my own covetousness reflected; I'm a sucker for small, hand-friendly artifacts, and these two were nice whether they had any antique value or not. When a quick exchange showed that he wanted less than $20 American for each, I counted a stack of greasy tugrugs into his hand, and pocketed the blue stone as surreptitiously as though it were dope. Ed did the same with the spoon.

Now, though, our friend wanted more. "I live in house. MONGOL house!" he sprayed. "Will show you house for twenty dollar. Show you wife, too!" I shook my head; apart from my doubts about his company, I didn't have another twenty to spare. He followed us disconsolately through the maze until we crossed under the tall red gates of the temple square, where he finally turned back, still trying out variations on his pitch: "Very old, *very* old, very *old* . . ."

Under the gates sat an old man, cross-legged, as perfect and elegant as "Very old" was tatty, basking in the sun. His white beard was perfectly trimmed, his robes immaculate. A round, fur-trimmed cap sat on his head. He puffed on a long-stemmed pipe, nodding a greeting to each entrant. Many of the younger ones bowed to him. His dignified smile was a blessing, warming us as we fled from the salesman. I stopped, like a tourist, to snap his photo; he acknowledged me momentarily by making a serious face and sitting up straight. He then politely refused a bill, resuming his distant smile.

The temples and monasteries in and around what you might call the religious area—Gandanlegchinlen Monastery, more familiarly "Gandan"—stand in Tibetan splendor in a huge barren square surrounded by acres of open space, like a parking lot. They lend color and architectural magnificence to the bleak scene, especially the Migjid Janreisig Süm, with its newly restored, one-hundred-foot, gold leaf-covered Buddha. Inside, their halls hum with activity—prayer wheels spinning, drums beating, and a constant background of chant. It's hard to remember, amidst all this activity, that the communist government, in addition to killing lamas, made a law prohibiting any "ongoing reincarnations" from 1924 until the collapse of the Soviet Union. The effect reminded me nostalgically of the high masses and Gregorian chant of my youth; the fusion of strange and strangely familiar was both comforting and enchanting. But for overall magic I preferred a much smaller temple to the south. Even in February's chill it looked like the temples in classical Chinese landscape painting, with intricate rooflines shaded by tall symmetrical pine trees. On the roofs perched a menagerie of biomorphic statues and ornaments— the golden deer from under the Bo tree, symbols of Buddhist enlightenment (which Mongolians will tell you are Mongolian gazelles) birds, fish, and many less recognizable animals.

And among them stood lines of even more interesting inhabitants—the city birds of Ulan Bataar. Ravens, the totem bird of my New Mexico landscape, dominated the scene. They perched alone atop the highest peaks of the multiple roofs, or cut through the throngs of lesser birds with sinister intent. The smaller crows, indistinguishable from ours by eye, perched everywhere amidst the hordes of pigeons, competing with them for the snacks thrown by pilgrims. A long trilling whistle diverted my eye to a structure of wire on one of the roofs. My pocket binoculars—the only possession I refuse to travel without—resolved into a bird a little like a raven, no bigger than a jay, with a bright red, downward-curving beak. It was a chough, the first "real" new bird—I couldn't count ravens, crows, and feral pigeons—that I had seen in Mongolia. Choughs are different from any American bird. They really do fly like their distant relative the raven, soar like hawks, dive and flare and rattle and roll. They don't mind people but they seem to prefer bleak, rugged landscapes—seashore cliffs, desert mountains, bleak plains—again, like ravens.

Then there were the pigeons, formally known as rock doves. They are much more interesting than most people think. A whole organization, based at Cornell University, The Pigeon Project, ex-changes research on the worldwide color phases of that ubiquitous bird. These ones were not the ordinary mix. At first I thought that the rainbow of colors available had somehow pinched to only two: the wild phenotype pigeon fanciers call "blue bar," with its gray-blue wings crossed by two black crescents, and a type that geneticists call "T-pattern" but that most people, laymen and fanciers alike, would simply call "black." This in itself was strange; amidst literally thou-sands of birds, wheeling in flocks that stacked up into carousels in the brilliant sunlight, I watched for an hour and did not see one vari-ation, no speckled "checkers," brown "reds," or pinto "pieds." I had never seen such a thing, and began to snap photos to document the phenomenon for Cornell.

Soon it dawned on me that there was something else going on. I had semiconsciously noticed that quite a few of the blue bars were smaller and paler than normal, and that, when such individuals were courted by the macho male rock doves, they edged away. The mys-tery resolved itself when a kid ran through the flocks scattering them into the air. Flushed, the smaller pigeons revealed that they pos-sessed shining white tails tipped with bold black bars, as striking as the startle patterns on the underwings of moths. They weren't com-mon pigeons at all; they were hill pigeons, *Columba rupestris,* an Asian high-country species. We would see their flocks feeding amidst the bare stones of the mountains when we left the city and its urbanized blues and blacks behind.

WE RESUMED WORK THAT AFTERNOON, VISITING THE MONEY changers, who did business in a building that seemed to have been abandoned. Inside, like many business buildings in Mongolia, there were no working electric lights, and most of the windows were boarded up. The place was full and noisy, with customers yelling over the sound of winter boots on the cracked marble floors. The money changers themselves worked behind a counter like bankers, though the lines, like those at Mongolian airports, weren't lines at all—you pushed, shoved, and shouted yourself to the front. Later, in rural airports and banks, we strangers would be helped to the front with full nomadic hospitality; UB, apparently, was too modern for this old formality. With difficulty, I detached my new "Big Face Money" (only modern bills were acceptable, we were told, because of the multitude of old forged bills from the Bekaa Valley in Lebanon) from the money belt I had been told to bring, and gave it to David for bargaining. I never used the belt again . . . it was too hard to get American bills in and out of it. (Mongolian bills—tugrugs, pronounced more like "tugrig"—are small and portable, decorated with handsome nomadic scenes. They almost universally smelled of mutton fat—money to frighten vegetarians.)

We then got tickets on MIAT, the Mongolian state airline, in the same building, after shoving ourselves to the front of the line and allowing Canat to make our demands. The airline flew to Olgii only twice a week. He was to fly on ahead, while we would join him a day later. That evening, driven from the Turkish restaurant on the square by the scowl on the Volkswagen-sized head of Lenin hanging over the tables like a bearded Wizard of Oz, we entered another one called "Fast Food," a Chinese restaurant run by a German chef, only to encounter Kent Madin. Mongolia is huge, but with so few people you will always run into someone you know. As we ate spicy noodles and washed them down with German beer, I laughed along with everyone, but felt hopelessly stalled between cultures. Maybe my mind, or my soul, was still strung out somewhere behind me.

Out in the freezing night, my mind flipped over. It came to me in my alcoholic buzz that this was more than the home of an ancient culture; it was a road map to the next century, an enjoyable but disconcerting nightmare, like a cyberpunk novel. Out in the freezing, black-fogged streets the tenth century passed through a mosaic of 1950s Russia and the Twenty-First. Soviet cars, Chinese Jeeps, and black-windowed BMWs and Mercedes roared past ponies on their way to eighties Eurodiscos with mirrored balls and restaurants glowing with silken tents. Ulaan Bataar was Stalinist sculpture, Japanese sedans, e-mail, and expatriates. The air stank of dung, exhaust, coal smoke, and piss, embedded in a fog so cold it froze your lungs. It was medieval; it was science fiction. And—I had to admit—I loved it.

WE HAD TWO MORE THINGS TO DO BEFORE WE LEFT THE CAPITAL the next day. I wanted to visit the Natural History Museum to see if they had any material on birds of prey or Kazakh culture, as well as to see the famous dinosaur fossils. And Ed had arranged with David for us to interview a young Mongolian who had worked with several American expeditions, to see if he wanted to join a trek across Mongolia with an American group the next summer.

The museum is an imposing structure; four stories high, lining several blocks just north of Ulaan Bataar's biggest square, Sukhbataar. On the day that I visited, a monstrous new black Chevy Suburban with those sinister black mirrored windows, the only one I ever saw in Mongolia, nearly blocked the stairs. I had to knock to get into the nearly empty building, and endure some complicated bargaining about checking my coat. But once I did, I had free rein of the place, including dinosaur halls, which is apparently not automatic. I wandered in, testing closed doors to see if any would open.

Most of the dead-end corridors resembled those in little old poorly funded US provincial museums, whose collections of animals had been made at the end of the last century. The specimens were lean and understuffed, with bared teeth and glaring glass eyes. A badger had been left in the sun so long its fur had faded to an albinic white; with its long, skinny, arched artificial body, only its scientific name remained to confirm its identity. The labels were in Japanese appliance manual English, if they were in English at all, though enough of them were in Russian to help with their identification. (I do not speak Russian, but studied it in high school; I can still read the Cyrillic alphabet phonetically, and remember some words.)

The funniest unintentional labels were in the bird section, where I knew enough to be a critic. Three identical immature saker falcons, similar enough to have hatched from the same nest, were labeled "saker," "peregrine," and "lanner." Although two of the three species occur in Mongolia, they don't look that much alike; if this were the current state of Mongolian ornithology, I had more sympathy for the irritable expat.

When I finally found the hall of dinosaurs, hidden around a blind corner on the third floor, it was a different story. The well-lit room extended up two stories to give the monsters headroom, and was filled with treasures. Mongolia has been producing amazing fossils ever since Andrews's expeditions in the 1920s, and it sometimes seems that only the surface has been scratched. Its sandstone cliffs have yielded monstrous carnivores, parrot-beaked herbivores, and more dino eggs than any other place in the world.

If you are interested in predatory birds you inevitably become interested in the current ferment surrounding the origins of birds and dinosaurs *as* birds. Despite the rearguard defenders of birds as something other than dinosaurs, it seems more and more that they are a mere (if successful) branch of the Theropod (flesh-eating) dinosaurs. The roadrunner is a dinosaur, as is the golden eagle and the hummingbird. Bob Bakker, the iconoclastic paleontologist who looks like a biker, calls the Tyrannosaurus "the forty-foot roadrunner from hell." It may have even had feathers, at least when it was young . . . and its ancestors may have flown! I can't help thinking that Roy Chapman Andrews would have been delighted to see his dinosaurs take on a fierce new life. (The fascination seems to work both ways; a recent photo of Bakker shows him holding a golden eagle in the manner of a Kazakh falconer.)

The source of most of the fossils contributing to the blurring of the lines is Mongolia or nearby China. I looked at *Oviraptor,* which resembles a huge four-legged carnivorous guinea fowl, and which was found guarding its nest against another birdlike raptor; at Protoceratops, with its macaw's head and reptilian body; at eggs containing embryos with delicate avian bones.

From one wall hung a pair of gigantic arms, tipped with sickle claws that could eviscerate an elephant: Dinocheirus. I had seen their image twice before: once in a dramatic photograph against a black background, menacing a Mongolian paleontologist who stood pensively between the claws, dressed in riding boots, a fedora, and a Mongolian duster coat, evoking memories of Roy Chapman Andrews; and again in the Natural History Museum in London, where a "life-sized" cast replica formed part of an interactive dino show. Although this display was less artful—the talons hung from heavy brackets in front of a window that looked south to Sukhbataar Square—it was far more moving: rough and raw, as though the talons had recently been wrenched from their stony matrix a few hundred miles further south. They were old and dirty, rough to the touch, and utterly real, not unlike the eagles' talons that I had so often felt in reality and in my dreams. Staring at them I could all-too-easily imagine the stains of dried blood, the stench of old meals, the cutting metal screech of their ancient battles.

Behind me stood the biggest carnivore of them all, *Tarbosaurus:* Central Asia's answer to T. Rex. If *Tyrannosaurus* was, as Bob Bakker described her, the ten-ton roadrunner from hell, this even bigger biped, with its four-foot jaws full of serrated teeth, could easily be seen as a great, wingless, toothed eagle, rampant on its stone base. To anyone who watches predatory birds, the dinosaur-as-bird/bird-as-living dinosaur equation makes instant intuitive sense, especially when you look at the big predatory bipeds. They must have moved like great stalking secretary birds, with brilliant eyes and bobbing heads; attacked in great bursts of speed, killing with quick strikes of head and jaws from bodies balanced on two legs; then ripped flesh from the bones of their fallen quarry with repeated flexes of their bowed backs, pausing to look left, look right, between bolting down hunks of flesh, even as their hollow-boned winged descendants do today. Their tails would have been poised behind them as a counterbalance, like a bird's stiff feathers, as they gripped their prey with taloned feet. Once again, I could almost hear the rip, the hiss, see the sideways flick of a hard jeweled head to discard an unwanted morsel. It was as though the old bones had resumed flesh, scales, eyes, perhaps even a crest of feathers, and were watching me. Maybe only a raptor aficionado could see it.

BACK AT THE HOTEL, THE INTERVIEW WITH THE YOUNG Mongolian gave me less scope for imagination. Ariunbat was a charmer, as easily articulate in English, including gen-X slang, as any twenty-something American grad student. He worked in the governmental press section, and had spent time in Arizona. He even looked like a Navajo, with fine features, straight black hair, and a thin aquiline nose.

At first he seemed a little uncomfortable about the project, which also seemed strange to me. For years, David has been obsessed with the connections between Central Asian and Native American people. Certainly the physical resemblance can be amazing, from Tibet across the Bering land bridge all the way to New Mexico. Much later, back in New Mexico, I would prompt an exchange between Canat and an Alamo Navajo friend, Paul Jones Apachito, on the similarity of contents and layouts between hogans and gers; photos of Paul's family hogan now hang in Canat's ger, and visa versa.

Some of the similarities are doubtless environmental; Navajos, although their old Iberian sheep resemble Mongol and Kazakh fat-tails, only became pastoralists after the Conquest. Some are odd. Mongols and several southwestern tribes make silver and turquoise jewelry, and use coral ornaments as well. Although Navajos and Pueblo people learned silversmithing from Europeans, the designs of Mongolian and Navajo bracelets can be startlingly similar; some time I later saw at the museum shop of an Ulaan Bataar temple (and could not afford) what could have been perfect pre–World War II "pawn" bracelets from the Navajo, nicer than almost any you can get today. And some similarities are positively eerie. A photo David took a few years before outside a Tsatsan reindeer herder village looks at first sight to be impossible: a clear color photo of a pre-contact Plains Indian teepee village. I am no anthropologist, but I cannot tell the design from western teepees I have been inside.

Still, this particular project seemed a little perverse: a big budget, carefully photographed and choreographed television program that would follow a bunch of politically minded Canadian Indians in a high-tech caravan across Mongolia, in search of roots and "spirituality."

For one thing, for all my irritation at New Agers, I was a little unsure if "spiritual" was exactly the word to apply to Ariunbat; "political," in several senses, seemed more appropriate. Much later a Mongolian who will remain nameless told me that Ariunbat was "KGB," which seemed less a literal tag than one symbolic of the old discredited regime. Once Ariunbat got going, he said nothing that would discredit that hypothesis. He spoke in sound bites. Free speech was "Okay for Americans. But now we have disloyalty, horror films, and pornography available everywhere." Democracy "brings in the Mafia." The free market was also a bad idea, producing poverty. The people had to elect a government that would clamp down on unnamed abuses of all kinds, that would commit itself to a "strong state policy." That he was advocating a return to the policies that had freeze-dried Mongolia since 1926 seemed impolitic for me to suggest. Still, he gave good sound bite: "Ulaan Bataar is not Mongolia. But Mongolia is only twenty kilometers away."

Even more interesting, in terms of authentication, was my first glimpse into what I would come to believe is photographic professionalism. I had already heard long discussions on how much faking was necessary, accepted, or even encouraged. In my own contrariness I had already decided to photograph Kazakhs in baseball caps even as David advised Ed to make sure they all took them off. But now I heard a suggestion that popped my eyes. "Would you consider," asked David, "growing your hair long for this? Maybe in a ponytail? Some of these guys from Canada have them, and it would look more authentic." Smiling, Ariunbat agreed.

I went to the minibar in the room for another German beer. Before first light, we were flying on MIAT to Bayaan Olgii, and this kind of authenticity was no longer any concern of mine.

EVEN BEFORE DAWN, THE ULAAN BATAAR AIRPORT WAS A scene of roaring chaos, with everyone doing what the *Lonely Planet* guide calls "the Mongolian Scramble." All flights on the state airline, MIAT, start between eight and ten A.M., whatever their destination, and Central Asians don't believe in queues. You can't assume you have a seat just because you have a ticket; the second does not guarantee the first. You must have your baggage weighed. And all of this must be done in a crush of bodies struggling for purchase, bearing up against the windows as though competing for space on the last flight out of Saigon. The crowd was composed of what I already thought of as the usual mix of centuries, sometimes in one person—for instance, a young Mongol woman in tight bell-bottoms and platform-soled shoes, was carrying a brand-new ZKK Mauser rifle in the "Monte Carlo" hunting model, made in the Czech Republic, slung over her shoulder, and under her arm its all-in-English factory box.

Only one flight to Bayaan Olgii was listed on the board, and it left at eight-thirty. Despite the push of bodies, Mongolian citizens are unfailingly helpful; when it became apparent that Ed and I had no idea what we were doing, helpful strangers wedged us in toward the front of the scrum, while others passed our baggage overhead to be weighed, including Ed's big-as-a-body-bag-and-twice-as-heavy duffel, full of camera equipment. An elegant young woman dressed in a fine wool coat and expensive boots called out to us in perfect English, asking us what we needed, and introduced herself as Ms. Mora Ichinnoron, a trial lawyer. She then began berating the officials in the window on our behalf, refusing to take any excuses. Still, it was exactly eight-thirty when we pounded breathlessly down the stairs toward the exit door.

"Bayaan Olgii! Bayaan Olgii?" I yelled, pointing at the runway. The single, and probably nonofficial, inhabitant of the waiting room pointed out at the runway, where a fat little Soviet-type jet stood, warming its engines. The sun was still below the horizon. We crashed through the doors and ran, baggage and binoculars flapping from our shoulders. We didn't even know if the cameras were on board.

We realized immediately *we* weren't meant to be. When we gasped up to the single official standing by the roaring plane, he shook his head when he saw our tickets and pointed back toward the terminal. "Bayaan Olgii," he said, firmly but not unkindly. "Bayaan Olgii."

We dragged ourselves and our heavy carry-ons once more over the greasy tarmac, panting, sweating, our faces freezing. As we reentered the hothouse atmosphere of the building, the first person we encountered was Mora, impossibly chic in her makeup and white silk scarf. "Don't worry," she said. "That was the *first* flight to Bayaan Olgii. Second leaves at nine-thirty. Your baggage is being loaded now. I am so sorry." We thanked her profusely, denied she had anything to be sorry for, exchanged cards, and agreed to meet when we returned. I promptly collapsed into a seat and fell back to sleep.

The real flight was far more relaxed, if no less daunting. The plane itself was one of those Russian jets, with one nearly bald tire and seat numbers scrawled on pot metal in Cyrillic characters, more messily than my handwriting. About half of the seat backs were broken, the overhead bins spilled luggage, and the heat, considering the climate, was intense.

All of which faded into insignificance beside the remarkable carry-ons. Many were something I would come to find ordinary in the next month: whole frozen sheep, or rather an entire sheep's worth of meat, bagged in its digestive system and frozen solid into a huge whitish mass as hard as granite. These fascinated me; the next one scared the hell out of me. Two sweet old Moslem grannies in head scarves were seated directly behind us. They beamed greetings at me as I adjusted my seat so it wouldn't collapse into their laps, each of which contained a large, red plastic five-gallon container of—could it be?—yes, *gasoline*. The stench was overwhelming. Two seats ahead, a fur-capped businessman lit what would be the first of about a pack of cigarettes. And surrounded by fumes, and drone, and polyglot babble, I fell asleep.

WHEN I AWOKE, THE GROUND BELOW SEEMED ENDLESSLY familiar. I sat on the plane's right side. We were flying west, which put the foothills, backed by mountains, to my right; while outside the left window the landscape provided endless plains, brown and relentless in their winter dress. The foothills became sharp-edged as they climbed north; snow clung in the shady spots, relieving their monotone browns. The higher mountains were composed of dark-blue trees, soft-blue shadows, blazing blue-white snows. It was Mongolia, not Montana or New Mexico, but it was exactly the right kind of landscape. Human traces were limited to tiny snowy scrawls of road, and here or there a camp of gers.

We knew there would be a stop for refueling; David had thought at Mörön, about halfway, which is *not* pronounced "Moron," but "Muuruun." As it happened the stop was in Tosontsengel, a bit further west. The difference was that while Mörön, the capital of a state, or *aimag*, is a small city, there was nothing visible at Tosontsengel but a closed air terminal, larch-clad mountains, and an arctic wind hard enough to abrade everything from the plane to your skin with particles of powder snow.

We had to get off the plane while it was refueled. Smart male passengers scrambled to the downwind fence, to empty swollen bladders before another three-hour flight with a locked restroom. I had envied the ones who had brought vodka, especially since the seats were murdering my back; now I wasn't quite so sure. Even without the vodka, it seemed to take a long time for my own bladder to relax in the numbing cold. I stood by the fence in the brilliant sun, steam rising off my piss and swirling downwind from my breath, with my nose freezing from the inside out, and my face glowing, and exchanged nods with my fellow travelers. I raised my eyes to the sculpted ice forests above, and felt utterly content.

BACK ON THE PLANE, THE GASOLINE GRANNIES NOTICED MY watch and, with gestures, asked for the time. I hadn't changed the position of the hands since Beijing. For some doubtless political reason both Beijing and most of Mongolia, for well over a thousand miles, were in the same working time zone. Now I remembered that it was time to set them to an hour earlier; crossing the border to Bayaan Olgii, the last and westernmost province of the two-thousand-mile spindle of Mongolia, finally put us into a different zone. I smiled and showed them what I was doing; they nodded back in understanding, and it occurred to me that maybe they had been telling me to do just that.

The Bayaan Olgii airport terminal was massive, cold, and dark, despite its tall windows. But waiting in line for us stood Canat, in his leather coat and sheepskin hat, grinning his familiar ivory grin. Beside him stood a shorter man whom it would soon seem I had known forever: Siassi. It is unfair to say that I "knew" Siassi quickly; it takes longer to know anyone who barely shares a common language than we had time to spend in all of Mongolia. David had warned me about him. Although he considered Siassi to be a decent driver, he had doubts about his drinking, and advised me not to let him drink during the day, nor to pay him much until we were leaving.

Perhaps David's attitude, which was certainly reasonable, came from differences in background—his and mine, not his and Siassi's. Our driver made an easy first impression as a rogue. He stood at about five-four, muscular and fat, with a broad face, copper skin, features far more Asian than Canat's. He affected a pencil-thin mustache and constant knowing grin that could easily metamorphose into a smirk. He inevitably wore a brown leather dress jacket, an English-style cap, and a cigarette stuck movie-gangster style in the corner of his mouth. I would find that he could be boorish, rude, conversationally aggressive; that he could down a 70 cl. bottle of vodka in three gulps, then go on to drink five more, and that he was not above a little chicanery and wheedling, not to mention provoking a bar fight and then leaving us to deal with it.

And yet, I almost immediately liked him, enjoyed his company, and would hire him again, not to mention recommend him as a driver for anyone from the west not caught up in the Puritanical mores of our present decline. Maybe its just my own roots, but I felt utterly at home with Siassi, felt I had met him before in the blue-collar men's bars of my Boston youth; in the cordwood-cutting, deer-poaching hills of my college days; in the southwestern small-town rancher's bars I still frequent. Siassi was a cowboy in town for Coors, women, and song; an Italian neighborhood guy; a "Meskin," a Navajo hell-raiser. Canat was a warrior, a gentleman, and a friend; Siassi was like my bad-ass kid brother.

At the moment I could know none of this, of course, but his manner still felt familiar. "Me, Siassi," jerking a thumb at his chest in a gesture that looked, again, like he learned it from an old movie. "Friend, David. *Good* driver." He picked up one of our smaller bags. Canat had already shouldered the heaviest. "You, Ed," he continued. "You, *Stev.*"

"No, *Steeve,*" I corrected. "*Stev,*" he corrected back. And so I was to remain.

IF I COMPARE ULAAN BATAAR TO A TOWN IN MONTANA, Bayaan Olgii, cold and golden in the late-afternoon sun, was at once superficially more familiar in its high-desert setting and far more exotic. It looked like Hollywood's idea of Tibet, minus the temples, and I loved it instantly. This city of almost twenty-thousand stands at an altitude of six thousand feet in a high dry mountain basin, surrounded by red-rock hills, backed in their turn by glacial crags. As we drove north toward town, commuters seemed to favor motorcycles or horses to cars, and when we actually hit pavement I saw my first ridden camel jogging past a Mercedes at a traffic light, a shaggy Bactrian with blackish-brown pelage rather than the pale color of the courtyard beast in Beijing. Breath and exhaust steamed in the clear chilly atmosphere.

Canat thought we should lay in supplies at what he called the "black market" while it was still light, so Siassi turned his Neva toward the outskirts again. (The car, which they both called "Russian Jip" rather than by its proper name, practically became a character in its own right before the trip was done. It was green—which I, being colorblind, promptly mistook for its opposite, confusing my guides—and looked a bit like a seventies vintage Toyota Jeep with its edges melted off. While it gave little concession to luxury, I'd buy one in a second if I lived in the Third World *chimbambas.* From my privileged "expedition leader" perch in the shotgun seat I could see everything, and brace myself with a hanging bar so that I didn't screw up my back too badly. We never got a flat, despite the absolute absence of pavement (and presence of big rocks) anywhere outside of Olgii City, and never bogged down. Fuel economy was more Japanese than American. And like most Russian machines—my utility-grade Baikal shotgun comes to mind—if anything does jam, the tolerances are not finicky, and a good mechanic can fix it with the next size bigger hammer.

The term "black market" is a residue of old planned-economy times, when the only place you could actually get anything was outside the state-sanctioned outlets. (That such markets flourished everywhere in Mongolia, even in those times, is a tribute to Mongol-Kazakh ingenuity and nerve.) It now boasts a proud sign over its pay-to-enter gate: "Bazaar." In the transition between Mongol *zakh* and the Turkic *bazar,* we were reentering the farthest eastern reaches of the west, from its back side.

The bazaar was a palace of dusty delights; the smell of beasts and meat roasting; stacks of fine goods mixed with plastic junk and exotic food, piled in jumbles and beneath awnings. Hats of red silk, and fox fur-capped piles of cassettes of Kazakh music with handwritten labels and bootleg western rock, both of which rang from competing boom boxes. We picked up instant coffee, hard candy in huge handfuls by weight ("For kids," advised Canat), and cigarettes for Siassi. Far more interesting to me were the animal products, some still on the hoof. Buckets, full of broken slabs of whitish ice, turned out to be simple frozen milk, and were not melting in the still sunny air. Lambs stood in bundles, bleating piteously, legs tied together. A camel groaned repeatedly as we passed by. Inside the bazaar's only solid building hung fifty or more blimps of frozen sheep flesh, like the ones I had seen on the plane. A wall of long sausages all seemed to reproduce the same exact curve. I asked Canat about them and he described the same curve with his hands: "Horse sausage. On horse rib bone."

In the end I bought only the candy, a couple of music cassettes for the "Jip," and some Chingiz Khan vodka. Having enjoyed Siassi's tapes on the way over, I asked him to pick me some. I already liked their galloping martial rhythm, which really does derive from the stride of a horse, although I would find that, despite the rhythm, they were more likely to be songs of love than songs of war.

Canat stopped in front of a stack of hundreds of identical little books, each bound in faux red leather. He gestured to Ed, who obediently asked: "So what are they?"

The dazzling grin again. "It is the works of Lenin. There are too many in this country, from when Russians were here. Now it is sold by weight, for toilet paper. We read Lenin—" he mimed study "—and then we *answer* him," miming that. "Good quality, too . . . you don't put your finger through."

CANAT WAS HORRIFIED THAT I MOSTLY WORE NO HAT; HE thought I'd die. Usually at home in the winter I wear western style, i.e. "cowboy," felt hats, which keep one's head surprisingly warm despite their lack of ear protection. I had bought a geeky synthetic Snoopy helmet from a good outdoor company, but when I saw myself in the mirror I looked so idiotic that I refused to wear it except to save my life. Ed had a sensible sheepskin hat, Turkmen style, very much part of the culture. He had also outfitted himself with a pair of Mongol suede boots in Ulaan Bataar. Canat didn't trust my expensive pacs, though they had withstood many Montana winters. "You need Kazakh boots, Kazakh hat," he advised. So we went shopping.

Canat soon found me a traditional Kazakh hat. It was made of fox skin, with a peak and backing of bright red watermarked silk. Fox skin flaps could be tied together on top, or left free to cover your ears. Another flap provided neck protection, or could be tucked up under the flaps. It fit perfectly and was the warmest thing I ever put on my head. I had doubts about the red color, which seemed garish, but Canat insisted that it was traditional. "Besides," he added, "eagle probably caught these foxes." I was easily persuaded to buy it, for about $20 American.

We left the bazaar to look for boots. Olgii's other stores were concentrated in still another suite of old government buildings. They were dark and unlit, like the money-changer's office in UB, and contained an amazing selection of goods. One was devoted almost entirely to more kinds of vodka than I ever dreamed existed, from foil-capped labelless local brands, through Stolichnaya (very cheap), and, amazingly, American Smirnoff (even more amazingly, the most expensive in the store.) The spaces between vodka bottles and cases were filled with endless cans of German beer.

But we could find not a single pair of boots for sale. Finally Canat suggested that if we drove by his house he would lend me a pair. Siassi was already eager to be home, but he agreed, if, we would hurry.

The outskirts of town turned, uncannily, into a New Mexican village. The resemblance was deep rather than superficial. In Carruthers and Lattimore I had seen flat-roofed adobe houses with rows of projecting beams, called *vigas* at home, under the eaves. I had seen no such thing in Mongolia proper, but suddenly I was surrounded by them. What's more, the fences around the yards were identical to our coyote fences—pales of skinny tree-trunks, with the bark still on, provided protection for goats, sheep, and horses. Only the blue doors—crescent and star on one, a mosque—looked exotic.

I pulled out a photo of my own humble four-room rock and adobe house, with its flat roof and backyard cottonwood, bare in a flat, cold winter light. Canat whooped. "You live in a Kazakh house!" he exclaimed. "We have trees like this. And *look*," he pointed at my windows. "You put plastic over your windows!" When we arrived at Canat's courtyard, it did look like home, even down to the calf nosing around his bare dirt yard.

Canat rushed in and came out bearing a pair of knee-high leather boots, cut rather loose in the leg, with red felt decorations protruding from the top. He insisted that I try them on, then and there. When I slid my feet in I realized that they enclosed removable felt liners, with the red band at the top providing a handle to pull them out. Despite the loose tops they fit as snugly as though they were made for me. They were as warm as my new hat. Their soles and heels, nailed from layers of leather, looked slick, but I soon found they gripped rock and even ice as though they, too, were felt. For the rest of my time in Mongolia I would wear them constantly.

The "flat" that Canat had rented for us was another surprise and delight. Outside, it was a grim Stalinist apartment block; squat, ugly, rectangular, with peeling paint and chipped concrete. The stairway was dim and steep. Canat opened the door after unlatching a typical tenth-century "Mongol lock," a wonderful hand-crafted flat object of copper or steel, with a push-in key. Inside, he flipped a switch, and the drabness of the architecture was instantly transformed.

It was as though we had stepped into a rich Bedouin tent, or an enchanted cave straight out of *The Arabian Nights*. Virtually every vertical surface was covered by wall hangings, in whirling abstract designs like those on Oriental carpets. The floors had real carpets, and the narrow boxlike beds were piled deep in throw rugs and brilliant pillows. Even the (broken) television had its embroidered cover. The only pictures were photo-calendars of Mecca. The mostly cotton material was humble, but the reds and golds and purples were dazzling. Obviously, the owners saved their display for friends and family. Later, I was to realize that this was no showplace, but a normal flat. Right now, all I felt was relief, and a sense of luxury I had never attained in the expensive hotel. Canat showed us the kettles, the coffee, tea, and a hot plate, and left with Siassi. He told us he would meet us at the "Disco Bar" for dinner, which I remembered as a pair of brilliant red doors across the street from the stores where we had searched for boots.

I took a bath, which worked well once I figured out that the hot and cold taps were opposite from home, something I would see everywhere in Bayaan Olgii but never saw mentioned in any guide book. Was it a Moslem thing? I availed myself of the sinful luxury of Ed's hair dryer, an appliance I never owned, and dressed warmly for my first night out in real eagle country.

The Disco Bar—sign in English again!—was tiny, even smaller than the Golden Spur back in Magdalena, but dazzling after the blackest streets I had ever seen in a city. It was definitely more a bar than a disco. Only a huge mirrored ball hanging in front of the inner door, and the thumping music in some utterly incomprehensible eastern European language, gave any indication of the first part of the little bar's name. Two sweet giggly young girls ran the whole show, which at the moment seemed to consist of two middle-aged intense smokers at one table and Canat, Ed, and me at the other. I ordered a German beer, and Canat ordered food. It was better than almost anything we had so far in Mongolia— dumplings, minced meat like spiced hamburger, diced hot vegetables, and a sort of potato pancake. Canat lifted his water glass—he would drink about three beers in the next three weeks—and toasted us. *"Kettik!"* He added, "Means: let's go!" I responded, in kind, and realized that we were here, in good company, smelling good food, and somehow at home. I felt consciously, for the first time: this is going to be *fun*.

The blackness of the city was nothing to the Stygian gloom of the flat's stairwell. It was like being deep in a freezing cave with the lights off, and the flat was four flights up. The Maglite, of course, was in the flat. I groped up through the utter darkness, hugging the hall, and felt for the lock, praying that I had the right apartment, since everyone apparently used Mongol locks. After I fumbled at the unfamiliar object with frozen fingers for what seemed like minutes, the key slid in: Home.

The beds were almost impossibly comfortable, the Kazakh pile of blankets and comforters on boards both firmer and softer than the hotel's sagging mattresses had been. I intended to read, but fell instantly into a deep sleep, the first good one I had had since we left California.

IN FACT, I SLEPT AS THOUGH I REALLY HAD COME HOME. MY dreams, which are often dark and turbulent, were comforting, silly, erotic, and adventurous. The only one I could remember beyond fragments was ridiculous and yet somehow comforting. In it, Libby and I rode with Canat at the head of a falconry and hunting caravan on the Mexican border, with hawks, coursing dogs, and hounds, and an amazing cast of border anachronisms; rancher and hound man Warner Glenn and his wife Wendy; my late (then-dying) mentor Floyd Mansell; my pal Dutch Salmon and his salukis, and a field of Kazakhs, Navajos, and Arabs. I woke ready for adventure.

WE HAD DRUNK OUR SWEET TURKISH INSTANT COFFEE BY
seven. At eight, Siassi was at the door. Despite David's warnings, he
didn't look a bit hung over. We carried our bags down and opened
the door to see not only our Jip but also the two biggest, blackest,
shaggiest Bactrian camels I had ever seen, tethered to a post by the
door. They were covered by enormous blankets of fresh-cut poles—
"firewood" said Siassi. It was a small revelation, the first of many:
camels deliver firewood to modern apartment buildings, where they
are left, parked.

When we arrived at Canat's, he ushered us in for a hot breakfast
of what to my palate could only be Cream of Wheat. His wife, Aika,
a tall beautiful woman with aquiline western features, served it with
a shy "Hello." Their children, son Bobsch, three, and daughter
Erkesh, seven, were less inhibited, as was Canat's cat "Boyo MacIn-
tosh," named after David and another photographer. I sipped tea
and peered through the steam at Canat's eclectic selection of objects, which included a cassette system that leaned heavily toward
Russian opera, Kazakh wall hangings, a rug with an image of an ibex,
and a new Russian-style masonry woodstove. Over the stereo hung a
reproduction of da Vinci's *Madonna*. Legos were strewn about on the
floor, and one wall featured photos of a younger Canat and Aika, as
well as a sharp-featured older man, in Kazakh dress and wearing
Russian medals—"My father."

I think Canat knew that we were impatient. With an approving
nod at my boots, he conducted us out, then climbed in back with Ed
and the mounds of camera equipment. I slammed the door, and
Siassi popped in a cassette. We drove through the not-very-heavy
morning traffic, headed north, and in less than five minutes, ran out
of pavement. We started up a long, pebbled slope under the shadows

of steep bare hills to our right, straight into the great open of Central Asia.

ON MAPS OF MONGOLIA, EVEN OF BAYAAN OLGII, ROADS ARE presented as bold unbroken red lines. When my stepson, Jackson Frishman, came back from Mongolia four years ago, he pointed to a spot where he had camped on his six-week long horse and raft odyssey through Hovdsgol. "Looks like it's not far from a big road," I muttered, perhaps a little disappointed.

He smiled. "Not only is it not near a main road, it's not near a *dirt* road. It's not even near a discernible *rut*. It's—sort of—on a camel route."

It wasn't any different in Bayaan Olgii. As we slowly ascended the long valley, the "road" resembled, and sometimes became, a braided dry riverbed, widening to a mile or two's breadth at times. It was composed of stones and cobbles, compressed into shallow ruts, sometimes highlighted on their edges by lines of dry, windblown snow. There was no traffic whatsoever; in the next five hours, the only wheeled objects we saw were one heavy Russian truck and one motorcycle, both headed toward us. Caravan debris, in the form of horse skulls, lots of camel hides, a random fender, a backbone, a muffler, was a bit more common, sticking out of the track's surface every mile or two. I suspected that similar artifacts and leftovers had been lodged in the road for centuries.

The landscape was vast and empty, southwestern in scale and barrenness, not unlike that in the stark corner where Arizona, California, and Mexico meet, with the same red-and-black roasted surface, burnished with "desert varnish," incredible vistas, and long slopes of eroded material beneath the ridges and mountains, sifted down by the winds and weathers of millennia. Except for one detail: the glimpses of snow on the highest ridges, the little drifts built up behind sheep bones in the track kept reminding me, against the visual impression, that rather than parched and hot it was *cold* out there; seriously cold, about five degrees above zero. And the light was different, too: gray around the edges, filtered through ice crystals. And, though apparently empty, the land was everywhere populated. The pepperlike dots on the far crests were not juniper trees, as they'd be at home; they were huge flocks of black and dark-brown sheep and goats. If you scanned the ridgetops through binoculars, sooner or later you would pick out a fox-hatted herdsman on a stout horse, watching you back; or an erect figure in the same sorts of places that would resolve into a carefully piled cairn of rocks.

I asked Canat about these, and learned something about my native deserts, where nobody raises sheep anymore. I explained that similar structures in Wyoming and Montana were referred to as "sheepherder's monuments." He replied that these statues probably had the same function back home as they did here. Which was? "Sheepherders build them to look like men. When wolves see them up above, they think they are men; they are afraid to attack."

Closer at hand lay long shallow mounds of stones, from grapefruit to head-sized. These were extremely frequent, and now I regret not counting them; perhaps as many as one a mile showed themselves on these old tracks. Canat told me that they were *kurghans* (graves), some more than a thousand years old, and that Russian archaeologists had excavated one not far north of the border, in Altai Siberia. He added that some thought it was bad luck to disturb them, although he himself found the science fascinating. (At that time, for fun, he was reading two paperbacks in English on scientific subjects: Matt Ridley's *The Red Queen*, and *The Wisdom of the*

Bones by Pat Shipman and Alan Walker.) Siassi, who could never let such a moment go by, loudly proclaimed himself "modern man—no superstition!" I soon found his bravado only existed inside the Jip— he didn't like stopping anywhere near the graves, never mind photographing them, and many of my snaps show the blur and fuzzy framing of shots taken from a moving vehicle. Later after seeing the reports and documentary on the "Ice Princess" tomb in the Altai, I wished that I had mapped, measured, and photographed the mounds more carefully. I can only advise archaeologists that there must be literally hundreds in Bayaan Olgii.[*]

Another stone object became visible when we turned around the outlying boulders of a new side canyon: a vertical sliver of rock, as tall as a man, decorated by layered white slashes of hawk "chalk." This, Canat explained, was a "balbal" (his pronunciation, though he corrected my spelling to "bulbul"). Bulbuls were "Turkish" battle monuments, sometimes grave markers. We would, in a few days, get to a place where we could see one with a face.

A few hours later we ascended a last slope to see a split between the mountains, carved as though by a giant's knife, falling away before us. "Is pass, to Bayaan Nuur; is 3,500 meters," said Canat. We turned off the Jip and got out to stretch, breathe, pee, and smoke. The road was at least a mile wide before it entered the canyon, the ground the boniest I had ever seen; pure stones. Libby was to announce when I returned, studying the fat sheep and horses and the utter lack of vegetation, that Kazakh livestock had obviously evolved

---

[*] In *Unknown Mongolia*, Carruthers states: "So amazing is the quantity of these grave mounds . . . that a portion of the district has earned the name of the Azkiezkia Steppe or "The Plain of the Dead." These monuments are to be found distributed in a wide area from south Siberia along the Urals as far as the volga. Their number in the Russian Altai, in Mongolia, and in the Uriankhi country is astonishing."

or been selectively bred to eat stones, and for all I know she may be right. I liked it anyway; as the naturalist Doug Peacock says of such barren places, there was nothing to cut down. The silence was as thick as earmuffs, the air as still as though it were frozen solid.

I walked out toward the rock buttress, breathing the thin air into the bottom of my lungs. A flurry of tiny birds with voices like broken glass blew up from invisibility between the stones at my feet, flashing white, whirling around and heading down-canyon. To my amazement, they looked to be snow buntings and horned larks, the spirit birds of "wastelands" everywhere, from Montana to New Mexico to 10,000-foot passes in Mongolia.

I turned back toward the truck once again and another movement caught my eye, high above. A little flock of larger, more purposeful birds were shooting through the white air overhead like animated arrows, as fast as birds could fly. Doves, I thought, but that didn't seem right. The conditions were too harsh. Then their pin tails caught my eye, demonstrating once again the similarity of desert dwellers everywhere. These were so-called sand "grouse" (probably Pallas's, *Syrrhaptes paradoxus*), pigeon-like oddities, inhabitants of some of the toughest ecosystems in the Old World, including the Kalahari and the Sahara; I had last seen their relatives in Africa.

As I reached the Jip, I saw the figure of a motorcyclist climbing from the pass toward us. He stopped to, as we say out west, "visit," as all people do in lonely places. He wore a modern version of the Kazakh hat wrapped in around his skull, and grinned through a mouthful of broken teeth. I commented to Canat that a motorcycle looked like a good transportation compromise between an expensive vehicle and an efficient but slow-moving horse. He shook his head. "You see his teeth? You drive motorcycle in winter for four, five years, the cold air will make your teeth like that."

We descended slowly into a deep red-rock canyon, where the frozen river ran compressed into a narrow *bosque,* with the road squeezed in on its right, suddenly narrowed to less than two car's width. Great bare trees, resembling, at least in winter, the cotton-woods at home, formed dense groves overhanging us on our left, or river, side. To our right the jumbled boulders began immediately, rising abruptly to tall cliffs hidden behind. Across the river the cliffs were clearly visible, utterly without a speck of vegetation, red and sandy-textured. Within minutes I had spotted my first falcon nest, deserted in winter but clearly marked by spaghetti-like white "noodles" of hawk chalk. I counted several more sites in the next twelve miles.

The southwestern comparisons can probably become wearisome, but the look of the river, bosque, and cliffs was entirely familiar until our first livestock appeared crossing a frozen river at an extremely deliberate, sore-footed shuffle: a camel. Ed banged on Siassi's seat back, leaped from the car, and began to stalk it. When he got his first shot he spotted a Kazakh adobe, what Canat called a "winter-spending place," nestled in the grove, and began to stalk *it,* ignoring the children gathering in the yard. The photo I took of Canat with my little point-and-shoot, exchanging scowls with me as we huddle beside the Jip, may reflect either my beginning discomfort with the dominance of photography or merely the fact that we were beginning to freeze solid.

We continued down the spectacular canyon, seeing new vistas of tourist-level "viewshed" at every turn, for another half hour. Then we rose abruptly out of the bottom into a sweeping plain, with livestock—sheep, goats, camels, horses—everywhere, and a whole new set of hulking dark mountains on the cloudy eastern horizon. Canat nodded his satisfaction. "Bayaan-Nuur, almost. But first, let us visit blacksmith."

We rolled, bumped, cresting and falling, over a river-bottom land-scape that by grazing and water action had taken on the semblance of a stormy sea, frozen solid. Hummocks two feet high, topped by thorny tufts of broom and thickets of taller thorn scrub, alternated with sandy-white washouts strewn with bones, until we pulled up in a half-circle to a ger with a bright blue door and smoke puffing from its stovepipe. Tree sparrows with black spots on their cheeks flitted around a brush arbor, while a shaggy shepherd dog approached with the purposeful step affected by guard dogs everywhere.

Jambitai the blacksmith was a short, swarthy man in modern dress, with a thin mustache. He welcomed us in while his children raced around yelling. The dog grudgingly backed up to allow us in, but growled when I held a hand out for him to sniff.

I'm not sure why Canat brought us to Jambitai's—could it have been for a bit of last-minute "training," a way to check our manners before we stayed with his relatives? I doubted, then, and doubt now, that Canat's mind works that way. More likely, a blacksmith and sad-dlemaker was something he wanted us to know about, and this one was on the way.

Nevertheless, I felt I must be on my best behavior. We were in-troduced, gave our best soft, two-handed Moslem shakes to our host, and sat on low stools around a table which was soon magically laden with what I would come to see as a typical impromptu Kazakh "tea"—bowls of soup-like salty "milk tea,"—more of sweet black "Chinese tea," flatbread resembling Navajo frybread, strong butter, rock-hard sour white curd that resembled Parmesan, and even harder red-orange cheese. We raised our hands, covered our faces with our hands in a rapid washing movement, and murmured "Bis-millah," then dug in. I remembered to hold my bowl to my face with both hands, and punctuate my conversation with polite slurps. It felt odd. (It is amusing to me to see a video Ed took a couple of weeks later where I am my usual gesturing, vocal, Italianesque self, while punctuating my animated conversation with loud, unconscious slurps from my now-naturally-held tea bowl.)

The food was welcome after the long cold drive; the tea not all that odd if I remembered Libby's advice, from when she was in Nepal, to regard it as soup rather than tea. The cheese-like curd was sharp, and as hard as the stones on the plains above; it would be a while yet before Canat saw my difficulty and advised me to soak it immediately in my tea.

I was intensely interested in my surroundings, and barely managed to converse abstractedly as I looked around the interior of my first "living" ger. But for the lattice supporting the walls, it could be the inside of a Navajo hogan, complete with a "modern" iron woodstove. The Kazakhs here sensibly use their gers as winter meat lockers, confining heat and living to their "winter-spending" log and adobe structures until the spring lambing (a date which would assume an enormous importance soon, though as yet I had no idea). Butchering—many sheep and goats, a horse and cow or three, though usually not yaks, which Canat described as "greasy"—was carried on in October, and the meat hung all over the walls, like anatomically correct art. The room was decorated with Arabesque blankets, chests, box beds, and wall hangings placed between racks of ribs. In front of our host was a nearly completed saddle, lacking only its silver decorations. To me, unversed in saddle history, it looked a bit western: deeper and more formed than an English-type saddle, but with an inverted metal loop in front instead of a horn.

Canat caught up on the news, then hurried us back to the Jeep. He wanted us to reach the village of his in-laws before dark. We bumped back up the plain and headed toward a twilight eastern horizon. In fifteen minutes, Bayaan Nuur ("Rich Lake") spread across the horizon, uncannily like the turn-of-the-century

Magdalena I had seen in old photos: rock outcroppings above, flat-roofed adobes below, "coyote" (i.e. wolf) fences everywhere. The traffic of cows, ponies, goats, and sheep thickened, and we began to see a few tracks and more Niva Jips. We forded a few ditches filled with broken ice and slow-moving shallow water, turned a sharp corner around an outhouse, and turned the engine off in the sudden silence of a walled yard.

The rest of the evening passed in a blur. My exhaustion had caught up with me, helped along by my first experience of *real* Kazakh hospitality. Canat's mother-in-law, a quiet dignified woman suffering from a toothache, directed her granddaughter and grandson in setting out everything we had eaten an hour before, plus flat, boiled noodles, a haunch of mutton, and German beer. Siassi went out briefly, and returned with a couple of bottles of vodka to add to the mix. There was hot water enough to really wash our hands, supplied by a little wood-heated tank. To our surprise, electric lights flashed on as the sun set; Bayaan Nuur itself, though not the outlying "ranches," enjoyed four hours of power a day. We ate as though we were starved, rolled out our bedding on the heavy wood-planked floor, and fell asleep instantly.

Morning came much too soon. I felt physically horrible—arthritic, dyspeptic, hurting everywhere. All my companions seemed to be sleeping like stones in the first, dimmest gleam of light. I pulled on my boots and a warm coat, and stumbled into the dawn. The sun had not yet risen; the courtyard was cold and gray and hard as stone. The only sound was a faint "carr" of crows flying as yet unseen overhead, and an occasional bleat from a goat or sheep out in the surrounding scrub.

I made tracks for the outhouse first, stomach rumbling and cramping. It leaned a bit sideways, like a joke outhouse in a western cartoon, and contained a slit trench bordered by planks in typical

Moslem fashion, rather than a seat. (Canat would later query me in great detail about the European-American preference for sitting on commodes when he began to plan his own tour company.) At the squatter's left hand stood a coffee can full of the works of Lenin.

All this didn't particularly intimidate me, though it took some engineering and agility to squat cleanly in the ten-below wind while wearing knee-high boots, long underwear, and a heavy coat. What did inhibit me, beyond the constipation and cramps of an all-fat-and-meat diet, was the six-foot pyramid of frozen feces thrusting up from below, festooned with the works of Lenin and pointed directly at my rear. I felt like a doomed victim of Vlad the Impaler.

Eventually, I answered Lenin without bothering to read him, and exited, little knowing I'd soon be nostalgic for this, the last "civilized" toilet I would see for some time. I wandered out, passed through a stone gate with a wood beam overhead, and started toward the river.

I was walking into the sunrise, but the ice crystals that routinely permeated the atmosphere allowed only a dim glow. My way wound through bristling hummocks like the ones we had driven over the day before. The "floor" was matted, chewed vegetation, studded with protruding rocks that tripped me up in the near-dark. Every few hundred yards multicolored fat-tailed sheep and little black goats shied away from my unfamiliar sight and scent. Behind me in the village, a dog barked with the regular rhythm of a metronome.

The river, under its casing of milky old ice, revealed itself suddenly under a four-foot vertical bank over which I nearly fell. In the slowly brightening rose-gold light it held an icy arctic beauty. Crows were beginning to trade back and forth between the bare cottonwoods on the islands and sandbars. The trees also held oversized basketballs of sticks which I realized were magpie nests, last seen in Montana. The clouds in the east were burnished, glowing behind the dark crags of the high mountains across the stream. It was so cold I felt the inside of my nose freeze.

I sat and breathed, watching for birds, feeling better and calmer. Predawn walks always improve the internal weather, no matter how bad you feel. Finally I turned back toward the village. The dinosaurian ridge over the town had just caught the first rays of the sun and was glowing gold, as though lit from within, against the bruised color of further ranges. Two magpies flew overhead in tandem, trailing shiny tails, like ribbons, behind them. Smoke rose above the huts as the sleepers came alive. I could hear the intermittent roar of a motorcycle engine.

As I started back, I realized with a mix of amusement and mild horror that the stones I had been stumbling over weren't stones at all; they were bones. Camel bones, horse skulls, unidentifiable bits of teeth, sheep and goat bones, finally a skin with the skull still attached. I was beginning to think of all of Central Asia as an immense ossuary, a charnel house of bones, from the great dinosaurian skeletons in the Gobi, to the tiny bones of foundling lambs under my feet. History, human artifacts, cobbles, bulbuls, graves, and camel skulls all fit together to form a pavement where the hard inhabitants walked, staying fat on rocks until they became stones themselves. No wonder the air was full of crows and ravens and magpies, eaters of the dead.

The thought stayed with me as I entered the courtyard. Waiting for me were a black goat, folded up atop the wall and regarding me with golden eyes and barred pupils, and a crow perched on the beam over my head, who didn't deign to move even when I raised my hand to stroke his tail. The feeling wasn't morbid—more like fatalistic and black-humored; like the grin on a skull. It soon vanished in the noise and bustle of breakfast (Indian tea, creamy buckwheat cereal) and the excitement of planning for our first "eagle hunt." But it would remain as an underlying theme of the entire trip, and has never quite vanished; I've never seen a place before or since where time's remnants are so visible.

The house was bright and cheery now, its decor and furnishings a mix of Kazakh, Russian, and Western influences. Color photos of horses and palm trees, posters of Black Sea resorts (the in-laws had been comfortable under Russian rule, the mother a geography teacher; though they were happier under Mongolian governance) vied with patterned hangings and fox and wolf skins, all of which Canat said had been caught by eagles. The most remarkable artifacts, which I had missed the night before, were two large Russian 1960s-style televisions in the corner, one wearing a brand-new VCR. It seemed incongruous at first, in company with the Kazakh outhouse, but then I remembered the tale told me by my friend Chris Francis, an American biologist who managed stream ecosystems for a billionaire's enormous ranch properties on two continents. A delegation of visiting Russian scientists had arrived and Chris was showing them around. One was amazed at the presence of a flush toilet in his office. "But of course," said his friend reassuringly "this is for office only. Even in America, he has no flush at home." We Americans take some strange things for granted.

IT APPEARED THAT WE DID NOT HAVE FAR TO DRIVE. THE house of Suleiman, the first of our eagle hunters, was in the village, or rather at its southern edge. It was becoming apparent that David's casual remark—"There are two or three eagle hunters in every village"—was not mere rhetoric. We were at the compound in five minutes. It looked, by local standards, extremely prosperous. Four or five elegant and well-maintained adobes stood at the foot of a red-stone bluff. Several long tailed little horses—I had already been warned not to call them "ponies"—surrounded a kneeling Bactrian camel, a flatbed truck, and a tractor. But I had eyes for only one thing, stepping down from the Jip's running boards and starting toward the culmination of my longings like a man in a dream.

She looked as big as a sturdy human dwarf: thick, broad-shouldered, dark as a storm cloud. Her hood had the double leaf-shaped loop I had seen in the old photos. Her curving bill was horn, her feet shining yellow stone, her gnarled knuckles bigger than mine, her two-inch claws a dragon's; a dinosaur's. Pale fluff fanned out over the white bases of her tail feathers. She stood relaxed, her talons spread over the top of a tractor's tire at the height of my waist, so that her head nearly topped mine. Her braided leash connected the heavy sheepskin bracelets on her feathered legs to the hub of the wheel. From her left shoulder sprang a tuft, a plume of cloudy feathers as insubstantial as the river trees had seemed in the dawn. And she was perfect, with feathers as edged and shining as metal—damn all the nay-sayers and detractors who had never been here! In the bright desert light, she glowed like a dark sun, as elegant as a living thing can be. She was worth traveling four thousand miles to see.

Everyone seemed to sense the significance of the moment, and let me stand, stare, and drink her in for several minutes. Ed seemed disinclined to photograph her on the tractor tire, but to me the conjunction seemed a part of the timeless magic of pragmatic, still-romantic Central Asia. Finally, I pulled out what Canat always referred to as my "little point-and-shoot" and snapped her portrait.

I turned to see a short, smiling man proffering his hand for a western-style handshake. "I told him again that you are American falconer. He is pleased that a falconer from so far away has come to ask him about Kazakh falconry, and hopes he can answer all your questions. His name is Suleiman."

R. Suleiman (I never found out what the initial "R," pronounced "ayr," stood for) was the jolliest man we met in Bayaan Olgii Aimag—not just serene and benevolent, but positively jolly; a pocket Falstaff, and a showman. He was also, even as a grandfather, the biggest dandy. At the moment he wore a bright blue synthetic pullover under a green velvet tunic, corduroy pants tucked into knee-high boots, and a remarkable hat. Its basic structure was the same as mine, with an even brighter red-orange silk peak, but it was topped with what looked like the same kind of plume that adorned his eagle's wing. And where mine had simple fox-skin flaps, his was resplendent in tiger stripes of fawn and shiny black: what Canat later explained was a "twenty-six-fox" hat, striped with the legs of up to that many foxes, for wear in the warmer weather of the Mongolian spring.

He grabbed my hand again, and pressed it against the eagle; first, along the keel of her breast ("He says she is not fat, but was getting fatter—he has tried to put her back in condition for you.") then, as dispassionately as a gynecologist, to the twin bones of her vent, her most intimate parts. "He says, look how close together bones are. This is very good." She sat stoically, neither flinching nor snapping, a demeanor I would find universal in the eagles of Olgii. Her condition, too, was interesting. The rumormongers had alleged that Kazakh eagles were flown nearly starving. If so, their keels would have a cross section like a hollow-ground knife's. This bird felt quite fleshy, if not, as Canat had said, "fat."

Our host had a Mediterranean's rapid-fire volubility. He ushered us inside, pointing out objects everywhere, and conducted us through three rooms (his house was considerably bigger than that of Canat's relatives) to one with brilliant blue walls that contained another eagle sitting on a perch. This eagle's throne was a tripod roughly carved from the base of a tree, and painted white. In the blaze of light from the window the simple contrast of colors was dazzling: blue walls, white perch, black eagle, floors of polished wood; stark and austere as a meditation room.

Up in the gloom under the ceiling was another kind of display. Suleiman grabbed my hand and pulled me over to see his collection, hundreds of pinned-up photos that ranged from images cut from magazines to Polaroids, all containing eagle hunters and many containing Suleiman himself. As Canat raced to keep up he explained that most were by an American woman photographer who lived in Paris, and gestured to me until I wrote down the address. He hoped I would send him some pictures, and insisted on my writing down my address, too.

A slender young man in a long black corduroy coat and a green hat similar to Suleiman's came into the room carrying the first eagle on his right arm* and a similar perch under his left. Canat explained that they were going to give the eagle a drink of tea.

A child brought in a teapot and some lump sugar which he decanted into a drinking bowl as Canat translated. "Suleiman says that it is end of season. He has not flown eagle for two weeks, so she is getting fat. But tea and sugar give her energy, so she will be hungry and fly." Suleiman put a length of rubber tubing in his mouth like the end of a hookah and made a joke. "He says it is the exhaust pipe." He put the end in the tea bowl with its melting sugar lumps and sucked it up. He inserted the other end in the eagle's mouth, emptied it (the bird shaking her head but otherwise remaining calm) then repeated the process.

---

* Kazakhs, like many eastern falconers, carry their birds on their right fist rather than the West's traditional left.

"Now he will take off the eagle's hood. She will vomit fat if she has any." Suleiman suited his actions to Canat's words and, sure enough, after a moment she gagged, brought up a little tea, shook her head, and wiped her beak on the perch. She then "roused," shaking down all her feathers, and looked alertly about at the falconers, the children, and the remains of breakfast as though a morning caffeine dose and purge were the most normal thing in the world.

Suleiman's apprentice Bakyt (pronounced Bakt), the young man in the green hat, repeated the process with his eagle. She was a bit older and fatter than Suleiman's, and objected by flapping her wings for a moment when Bakyt pried her mouth open, but sat happily enough when he removed her hood. When she, too, was empty, the hunters rehooded the birds, took them up on their thick right-handed gloves, and beckoned us outside.

The courtyard was a bustling scene of organized chaos, with the usual mixed-centuries feel. The camel, which had risen, was beckoned to kneel so its rider could mount. Horses stood at attention as Suleiman gave brisk orders. Hunters slung Soviet-era .22 training rifles and single-shot 12-gauge Baikal shotguns. Siassi fired up the Jeep and popped in a cassette that rang out loudly in the dawn; that same Kazakh music, with the rhythm of a galloping horse. Suleiman pointed to a crested butte about a mile away, red-gold in the morning light, and Canat translated: we would climb the rocks and sit on top, while the younger hunters beat the plain below.

We let them get a bit ahead so Ed could film them riding by. I was exhilarated—the whole scene seemed perfect. In fact, a little too perfect. I felt as though I were riding through, living through, a movie. It was the soundtrack, of course. *Homo postmodernicus,* by whom I mean everyone my age and younger, expects one. I had a sudden fierce wish to be riding out, hearing only hoof beat, jingle, and wind-whistle. It was not to be. Later Canat would tell me that if I wanted to ride I must come early enough in the season to pick a horse; all others are turned out to pasture, and there was not enough time available during our flying visit to catch horses.

The camel's gait as we passed was utterly alien, a shuffle of legs combined with a back-and-forth motion, though he had no trouble keeping up with the swifter-looking horses. I commented to Canat, who said that camels were ideal for falconry: "Very smooth and very up high." The second was obvious; the camel rider's head topped that of his horseman colleagues by two feet.

We pulled up at the foot of the ridge to film the horsemen coming in. Suleiman gestured grandly from atop his little white stallion, pointing his crop to the top of the crest. "He says he will ride to the top." *Ride?* It looked like a hands-and-knees scramble for an unmounted man, but before I could comment Suleiman and Bakyt pointed their horses uphill and trotted straight up the rocks. I followed more carefully, holding on to the scanty vegetation to keep from falling.

The view from the top was enormous. Red plains flattened out as far as the eye could see. Snowy mountains, the high Altai, fringed the southern horizon, while the black hills of Uvs reared up past the river thirty miles to the east. All was eerily clear and still, save for the riders and footmen beating the brush below. Suleiman and Bakyt and their eagles sat companionably side-by-side on the two highest boulders.

And, for the next two hours, nothing happened. The hunters sat with a hunter's calm, which flowed into me. Once again, my soul had caught up with my body, and being an eye in the Mongolian mountains suited me just fine. It was warm in the sun, but the situation made us alert rather than sleepy. Canat talked quietly, querying me on the etymology of "flush": "Is it the same word? Rabbit flushed.

Suleiman's son flush rabbit. We flush *toilet?"* But mostly we sat and watched. I sensed that Siassi and Ed were getting a bit restive, but this was what we were here for.

Finally and suddenly, a hare* popped out of the thin desert scrub below, well off from any beater. Suleiman unhooded his bird and pointed her toward the running speck. She lowered her head and stared, bobbed her head, stared again. She shifted her feet, lifted her tail, and deposited a small amount of liquid droppings to lighten her load, launched . . . and flew thirty feet to a spire below. Instead of continuing, she watched intently for a moment, then sat upright. She looked back at Suleiman, fluffed her feathers, roused, relaxed, and began to pipe plaintively in his direction.

No falconers need a translation for those actions: sorry, too much work. I grinned and spread my arms to Suleiman to say, no problem, been there, I understand. He grinned back. It would take at least a few more days of dieting, or easier and more tempting flushes, before his bird would be "on" again.

We climbed slowly back down. As Ed wanted to get some action shots to the lure, Suleiman left the eagles on the ridge under Bakyt's eye; birds, especially heavy ones like eagles, will fly eagerly at the easy lure for a reward even when they are too fat to hunt.

Down below, Suleiman produced a week-old half-frozen dead hare from his bag, which gave Ed an idea. Could he possibly wear the dead rabbit on his head, and shoot the eagle coming in?

I bit my tongue, not knowing whether to laugh or try to answer reasonably: *these things kill WOLVES.* But Canat's look of horror probably exceeded mine. I reminded Ed of tons of pressure, of wolves,

---

* Although Canat used "rabbit" and "hare" interchangeably, every lagomorph I saw was a hare: *Lepus capensis*, the brown hare, now considered one species throughout Eurasia and Africa. They looked like the American black-tailed jackrabbits, *L. californicus.*

deer, and travelers' tales, and persuaded him to shoot from a safer distance, say two or three feet past the carcass.

Suleiman galvanized into action. It was impossible to think that he had never been filmed before—he was a ringmaster, a clown prince, every inch a showman. He swung the lure until the bird launched herself, then dragged it along the sand, screaming like a dying rabbit. He dropped the lure to point at the soaring bird, calling "Kukai, Kukai!"—his wife's name. He then turned to the camera, gesticulating, calling David's name, mine, Ed's, Canat's, even Siassi's as he pointed at each of us. Later he would tell me that he wanted to remember all our names when he saw the video. He screamed "Kukai" once more and the eagle skidded into the lure, feet forward and crest up, a domestic dragon. He dragged her a few feet to simulate a fight, still screaming, and dropped the cord again, smiling back at us.

As Ed filmed her gobbling her tidbits, Suleiman turned toward me and asked a quiet question: "He says, do you fly two falcons together?"

"Falcons, yes. Eagles, never!" I didn't think anyone in the west ever intentionally flew anything that big and possessive in a situation that would tempt her to retaliate, though I had heard horror stories of accidental eagle brawls at field meets in the Czech Republic. Suleiman just grinned again, beckoned to Bakyt, and began to pull on the eagle-encumbered lure, making the dying rabbit squall again and stabbing his glove toward the ridge. As "Kukai" bristled I could see a speck enlarging against the clear blue sky: Bakyt's bird, coming in. She circled uneasily, then landed lightly beside the lure instead of slamming it. After a moment the first eagle moved over and they began to feed, side-by-side. Suleiman grabbed my hand and pulled me in, encouraging me to stroke the birds, to fold an outstretched wing, finally to hood up each. They were calmer than dogs, calmer than sweet-natured peregrine falcons I had reared from ten-day-old fluffballs.

We watched Suleiman and Bakyt work their eagles for the camera for an hour, then repaired to Suleiman's for a question-and-answer session. I had a prepared list, and had already thought up a dozen more. He led us into his "study," with golden afternoon light pouring in through the windows like honey, offered me an unfiltered Russian cigarette and a shallow saucer which he filled with local vodka, and raised his hand in a toast. "To American falconer, who has come so far to see our eagles." I reciprocated with *"Allahu Akbar,"* which made him roar in a slightly horrified delight. "He says maybe," Canat said smiling, "we should not ask Allah to bless our vodka." I bowed to indicate I understood.

He took a knobbed ibex horn down from a peg on the wall and rubbed its curve across his forearm. "Is good for tired muscles, like when you carry eagle all day," explained Canat. Suleiman rubbed his own limbs, then extended my arm to bear down on it with the marblelike lumps. It felt good. He smiled, sat back, and invited my first question.

"I notice that these two are still young eagles." (That is, less than breeding age, about five years, with white at the base of their tails.) Do you take them from the nest, or do you take young, hunting, first-year birds; what we call 'passage' birds?"

His bird was two years old; Bakyt's four. Both had been taken as nestlings. He preferred such because they "talked"—that plaintive food call, which we had heard. Such birds are "like your child." Passage birds were good fliers, but not as trustworthy. They had to be trapped before they were four, else they were too hard to train. The best young were taken from the nest in the middle of July. If one looked feathered out, like an adult, and the other still showed down, the feathered one was the one to choose. (This made good biological sense—eagles will feed one chick preferentially over the other if food is scarce, until the larger chick eats the other. The phenomenon is known as the Cain-and-Abel strategy, a bit misleadingly since "Cain" is virtually always female.)

He described in detail the qualities of a perfect eagle. First, I had to see, he considered that here in the Altai were three "kinds": the Altai white-shoulder; the Hovda yellow; and the valley, or "oil," black. (All would be considered simply golden eagles of the Asiatic race by the westerner or ornithologist.) His was a black. They were all good, but the white-shoulder a bit stronger. Its shoulders were not all white, he added; just a few feathers. Regardless of breed, all good eagles should have long toes, the better to enfold their prey. The barbs on their feathers (he indicated by running his finger down one) should be thin. There should be four visible joints to each toe. Eleven to thirteen tail feathers were best.

Different eagles had different eyes. The best, he said, were "very strong—like yours." (Mine are green-brown, for the record—actually a common Kazakh color.) Some had eyes the color of a cigarette filter, which he called "yellow." These could catch other eagles! Whatever the color, eyes should be deep under the brows—"like yours," again. The bill should be narrow. If you put your hand around the eagle's leg "it should feel like one bunch." His and Bakyt's eagles both had excellent legs.

Did I remember feeling his bird's vent bones? His was very good—if you could only fit one finger between her vent bones, she would be strong.

How much did his eagles weigh? This was of interest to me because it was alleged in the west that the reason that Kazakhs could take such large quarry was that their eagles weighed twice as much as ours. The two outside looked big, but not *that* big. He answered that they could weigh 8 kg. or more when they were very fat (and not flying at all) in the summer; right now his weighed between 5 and 6 kg.—what we'd consider on the high side of typical weight, but hardly a monster.

A PERFECT KAZAKH EAGLE, WITH SILVER ORNAMENTS ON ITS
HOOD AND AN "UKHU" (EAGLE OWL) PLUME ON ITS WING.

SULEIMAN DIRECTS THE HUNT.

TWO EAGLES ON THE LURE.

"TEA CEREMONY"—GIVING BLACK TEA TO SAILAHAN'S EAGLE.

MANAI SERENADES HIS EAGLE.

KHAIRATKAN RIDES TOWARD ULAAN HUS; ALTAI MOUNTAINS ON
THE SIBERIAN BORDER IN THE BACKGROUND.

FOX SKIN.

RIDERS WITH EAGLES—HUNTING, WITH HOODS OFF.

LIBBY CONTEMPLATES THE INSIDE OF A CAMEL HUMP.

KHURGAN (TOMB) NEAR MANAI'S.

MANAI'S HOUSE—WOLF AND FOX SKINS HANGING.

Did he or others fly the smaller males, *sarsha* as he called them?
Some did. They were good for rabbits, but what would you want to
put on your saddle, a fox skin or a rabbit skin? He warmed to the
subject. A good eagle, he said, should take between twenty and forty
fox in a season. In the old days a fox could be traded for a sheep,
and a really good eagle could keep a family fed. Now, to sell a fox
skin for money was not important, although you needed fox skins
for hats. He trained eagles because it made him feel younger, and
very wild.

Did I know how to catch foxes? You could hunt them from above,
as we had today, or flush them from horseback. But you could also
call them. I sat fascinated as he produced a "dying rabbit" squall
from his throat, much more subdued than the one he had used to
toll in the eagles earlier. "Varmint" shooters in the western US use
wooden or plastic calls to make the same sound; Suleiman just used
his voice. He opened a drawer to reveal a trove of falconry "furni-
ture"—hoods, paper hood patterns, feathers, leather, leather working tools—and removed one with a wooden bar hanging from its
chin strap. I had seen this feature on the one David had sent me, and
been unable to explain it.

Canat translated: "When fox gets close, eagle must be quiet.
Eagle hunter does not take off hood until fox is very close. So eagle
hunter turns handle"—he mimed pressing in the bar—"and eagle
can breathe, but not scream. It is . . . *silencer!*"

I asked about training. Like all good falconers, Suleiman made it
sound absurdly simple; the intuition, attention, and ability of the falconer to observe make all the difference. For the first month of
training after the bird is fully grown, the hunter feeds her all the
food she wants so that she does not get frustrated. But all this food
is high-protein, low-fat sheep's lungs. What's more, as in the Medieval west, it is "washed"—soaked in cold water for several minutes

so it loses even more nutritive value. All this time you handle her constantly, pick her up and put her down, hood and unhood her. Some "old school" falconers, he added, drench the *bird* in cold water or stand her on ice. He will not do this; he loves his bird. Such birds will be too weak in cold weather. These are the ones who need rabbit skin mufflers.

Then give her one flight to the lure, followed by one flight to a captive hare. Finally, give her a chance at an easy, close up fox; and go hunting, easy as that.

The shafts of light got longer and redder as we sipped our vodka, smoked more than I had done in years, and handled the equipment. I held hoods crusted with silver ornaments, as though Navajos had become falconers, and carved wooden perches and arm-support saddle crutches (baldachs) that Suleiman himself had carved with images of foxes and birds. Every so often he would laugh at a query and Canat would say "He says, Stev is testing me to see if I am a real falconer. I will ask him a question now." He was particularly interested in falcons, like the saker-gyrfalcon hybrid in my photos, which he called *shunkar*, and how they flew. I told him most American falconers flew them high, stooping on such quarry as ducks from above, but that you could also fly them on hares, twisting and striking the fleeing quarry again and again until it was motionless. This seemed to appeal to him more than the bird flight, and he told Canat that he knew someone who did this; alas, he was away hunting wolves (with a rifle, not a saker!) I wondered how you trained horses to accept eagles—I had noticed that one of the youths would walk on the horse's right side, with the eagle flicking into its face with her wing. It's easy, he said: Kazakh horses are very calm, very kind. With *Mongol* horses it would be dangerous; they are "very angry."

We drifted into folklore. I asked about the filmy plumes that adorned his hat and the eagles' wings, and he gestured at a couple of the silent young watchers in the door. They returned in a minute bearing the entire skin, wings, and talons and all, of a huge smoky-gray and tan owl, an *ukhu—Bubo bubo,* the eagle owl, an even larger and fiercer relative of our great horned variety. This, he explained, was the only bird that could kill an eagle, and even then only at night. By putting the plumes on the eagle's wing, they gave her some of the owl's power. The talons on the skin were an inch long, curved, black, and razor-edged, coming out of fluffy feet like a tiger's claws.

I remembered Patrick's question: how do you train the eagles not to eat your kids? I wondered if such placid birds as Suleiman's were ever a threat to anything but foxes and hares. Oh yes, he replied. Other quarry, such as wild cats, wolves, and wild goats and small deer, of course. He, too, had heard the snow leopard story. But, if the trainer were careless, or did not work closely enough with his bird, they were dangerous to domestic stock and children. Children? Yes! He knew of one whose eagle veered off, too hungry, and killed his eight-year-old son . . . "ripped his heart out." (Canat added later that, for revenge, he didn't kill the eagle; he cut its talons off and released it to starve.)

Finally, as we rose a bit unsteadily to leave, I asked him how long the eagles lived. Very long, he answered gravely. He knew of one very poor young falconer who kept one for nearly thirty years. I was not sure if this was a real or legendary character, especially when he added that the unfortunate man had to ride a yak when he went out hawking, but when he added that it had made nests and laid eggs at least twice, I believed him. He added that this was not customary, or right; that you should keep an eagle no more than five years, ten at the longest, then return her to breed. The implication was that yak-man was so poor that he feared losing his only source of income. Further, if you ever had "a very dangerous sickness" it was your responsibility to fatten your eagle up and let her go.

We adjourned to the sunny courtyard, slightly light-headed, for a final round of photos. Suleiman ducked back in for a moment and returned with a cluster of objects between his hands. I extended my own, clasped together to receive, first, a brand-new leather hood for a male eagle and, second, a twist of paper full of ukhu plumes, bearing his seal in ink. When we returned to the car, Canat told me that he hoped that I had enjoyed Suleiman's company as much as he had mine; that he was a good man, a good eagle hunter, and that he was "very sensitive." I had, but one thing bothered me. It was increasingly apparent that we had come very late in the season.

THAT NIGHT, BACK AT THE HOUSE, WE AGAIN (FOR THE fourth and, when guests appeared out of the dark, a fifth time*) enjoyed what seemed to be half a sheep, plus horse sausages. The entertainment was novel: Mongolian TV game shows, disco, appliance ads; followed by videos of unreleased American and European action movies with Russian dubbing. (Russian dubbing consists of one man's shouting all the dialogue in different voices, while the English or French original sound goes on in a murmur underneath.) When we finally retired to the floor, I slept like a stone.

I TOOK MY USUAL MORNING WALK, DODGING THE BONES underfoot, watching pairs of magpies fly silently through the predawn

---

* Guests appear out of the void wherever you are in Mongolia, no matter how remote, or how late the hour.

sky. The ice on the river had not yet broken up, but a rim of clear, thin ice was beginning to surround the thick white crust where it melted and refroze every day. The signs were subtle, but spring was coming, an irresistible fact that was beginning to worry me.

For once, there was activity in the courtyard. Canat and his nephew were using a two-man saw to cut logs for the stove, and his mother-in-law was stirring a bucket of evil-looking black sludge beside a fresh cow skin that I had missed on my way out. Between strokes, Canat explained that they had butchered a sick calf yesterday, and that the old woman was adding its blood to the "animal food." *Blood?* The slurry did indeed look, now that I thought of it, like blood and stove ash. I shook my head; cow vampirism was no weirder a theory than rock eating to explain fat stock in a freezing desert.

Today our plan was to visit a very old man with a very good eagle, one that had already surpassed the thirty-fox mark this season. Sailanhan's house was uncannily southwestern: a rectangular adobe house with vigas on the edge of the river's bosque, with the white-capped mountains of Uvs province rising behind, glowing under the brilliant morning light.

Sailanhan's granddaughter, in one of the bright-yellow American caps dreaded by photographers, greeted us in the yard. Sailanhan himself greeted us at the door with a traditional two-handed shake. He was thin and ancient, almost too-picturesquely resembling a Mongolian sage, but with a merry twinkle in his "ancient glittering eyes." His eagle was even bigger than Sulieman's, like the berkuts of legend, as she shifted her grip on her perch in the screened alcove on the sunny side of the house. With Sailanhan's permission I felt her keel, and my heart sank. She was as fat as a Thanksgiving turkey.

Sailanhan, who looked to be in his eighties, was on the other side of the generation gap from even Suleiman. He was old enough to remember being a Kazakh before the Russian and Mongol communists tried to erase the past. He knelt before the low table rather than sitting on a stool, as did his neighbor and friend of the same generation who joined us for tea. Although his granddaughter wore a cap, ponytail, and US-made jeans, she served the tea and retired; though whether she was being a traditional Moslem or just bored with the elders' conversation was impossible to tell.

Sailanhan served me at the head of the table and presented me with a knife as Canat spoke to him, and then to me. "I told him you will cut the meat like a Kazakh and eat like a wolf." Of course, the tea came with white and red curds, a leg of mutton, a bowl of homemade butter, another of hard candies. The food seemed (even!) stronger; the onions sharper and older; the butter saltier. The horse sausages were heavily spiced, and encased in a thick rind. It was good, but very powerful, and I hoped I wouldn't regret eating.

Finally I cleaned the knife with a twist of Lenin paper, handed it back to my beaming host (that I knew enough to clean it seemed to delight him) and began the interview. First, I wanted to know, was the season over? Was that why his bird was so fat?

The answers made me a little easier in my mind. Most eagle hunters, he said, stopped hunting at the beginning of lambing season, both for the obvious practical reason and because the furbearers—fox, wild cat, wolf—began to shed their prime winter coats. But he had stopped because the last fox his bird had caught, nearly a month ago, had bitten her badly on a toe, and he wanted to give her time to recuperate. Further north, or south in the Altai, where we hoped to go, falconers were still hunting. He was sorry that he could not show us his bird flying at quarry, because she was exceptionally bold; she usually flew *past* the fox, then turned to meet it head on. ("Only weak eagles catch foxes from behind.") It was only when her last flight had gone on too long that she grabbed the fox from the rear, so that it could turn and bite her foot. The ability to fly that strongly once again argued against the pessimistic criticisms of the Kazakhs; no "starved" bird could fly strongly enough to pass the fox and stoop from ahead. I still wasn't sure I believed it, and it would be two years before experience confirmed his statement.

Sailanhan's command of lore, knowledge, and legend also marked him as being of another generation. His "eaglery" was a mixture of legend, dogma, and efficient practice. He spoke of "Chor," the first Kazakh eagler, whose eagle was called "Lightning," an exception to the usual Kazakh custom of *not* naming birds. He did not know when Chor had lived, but thought it was in ancient times. Sailanhan only flew birds raised from nestlings—"some men trap adults because they can't find young ones." Were there any good reasons to take an adult? Yes: "passage" birds will come to only one person, and will not attack dogs, livestock, or children. You must be more careful around nestlings. He thought that "Altai whites" were *not* strong. "Blue" eagles (his was blue, so called because of her beak color) were much stronger. There were also "cross" eagles, perhaps half vulture, he did not know.*

I passed out photos of my own hawks. He identified the gyr-saker cross as a "pure" shunkar, i.e. a gyr**, and a dark hybrid male I once flew as an *itilga*—an Altai saker male. My peregrine was *lashan* or *karshiga*. He surprised me when he told me that, in his youth, he had flown sakers at hare and duck—the first Kazakh I had met who had personal experience with birds other than eagles. He laughed when we both simultaneously mimed the rolling repetitive strike of a falcon chasing a lure.

---

* This is of course folklore—vultures and eagles cannot interbreed.
* * Gyrs and sakers may be subspecies of the same species. Mongolia has "real" sakers, wintering arctic gyrs, and the Altai falcon, a large dark nesting race that may be an intergrade. My bird was gyrfalcon-colored.

Two young men had appeared while we talked, and waited silently while we finished. While his granddaughter cleared the plates, Sailanhan showed us his treasures—hats, fox skins, and three beautiful bird pelts; a pheasant's, a ruddy shelduck's, and one from an Altai snowcock, a kind of chukar the size of a turkey hen. When I asked him if his bird had caught them, one of the young men stepped forward touching first the muzzle of his Russian .22 rifle, then a hole in the bird skin. *His* shot. Above the skins and wall hanging were two pictures. One was obviously a robust Sailanhan of, perhaps, fifty, with an eagle and a twenty-six-fox hat. To his left was a very old photo of a man wearing a sort of white turban, with an elegant pointed white beard, and an enormous eagle: Sailanhan's father, who had taught him all he knew.

The photo session was a bit of a joke. The young men dosed the eagle with tea to give her enough of an edge so that she would bother to fly at all. Sailanhan, mounted on a beautiful, fat little pinto, rode endlessly back and forth on the still-solid ice of the river, occasionally calling the eagle to fist or fox skin. I felt as bored as they looked, and wandered off down the river, looking for birds, while Siassi smoked and Canat assisted Ed. A pair of choughs courted in the still-bare cottonwoods, whistling sweetly. They were like tiny crows or ravens, with blood-red bills. (In fact, Siassi, who was becoming a walking dictionary of bird names, called them *chowarga,* little crow, from *khorga,* crow.) Spring was swelling in the buds and under the ice, and I was impatient to get on, to see some real hunts before it was too late.

We returned to the house for another tea, this one mercifully without mutton, and, unusually for afternoon tea, without vodka. The neighbor presented me with an ermine's case-skinned pelt, and Sailanhan gave me another set of ukhu feathers. We told tales, finally turning to the subject of eating strange things. I said that I thought sausage with bones was, well, weird. Then Ed claimed to have eaten a piece of human flesh when he was filming the Yanomamo in South America. Canat translated before I could stop him, the two devout Moslems recoiled, and I buried my face in my hands. After a moment, the demands of hospitality reasserted themselves. Still blushing, I presented the old men with battery-powered head lamps, a suggestion of David's that they both seemed to appreciate. I wanted to be out of there quickly, instantly, *now*, before any of us visitors said or did anything else.

BACK "HOME," WE ATE THE USUAL AMOUNT, AND SAW THE usual television. I drank more vodka than I was used to, and added about three German beers. I woke in the middle of the night with heartburn, a swollen belly, aching joints, and a head full of fear and doubts. Too late, too late, too late in the season; too late in life. Why didn't I try this in, say, my twenties? Why was I trying to emulate all my legendary heroes, most of whom, to quote my late partner Betsy, "were born richer than God," when I was forty-eight, penniless, and in debt, and still hemorrhaging money into the Mongolian vacuum? Was there any market, any need for this information in the world where I lived? Did the Kazakhs need me? Did I think my words were a kind of tangible immortality, for me or the eagle hunters? Was I writing against fear, or the void; or because nothing seemed real to me if it were not frozen in words? Was I going to die? Would I ever shit again?

When I could stand no more, I went out into the freezing black immensity of the Mongolian night, my flashlight's beam showing me the way to the toilet. The ground fog was impenetrable, the only sound the barking of a herder's dogs, the bleat of a goat. What in God's name was I doing here? Squatting over the trench provided no relief, physical or existential. I stared at Lenin's works with loathing, and decided to walk to the river.

Solvitur ambulando. As I stumbled across the frozen ground, other words came to comfort me, even as my own whines faded in my head; writers' words, like T. H. White's justification for writing his unlikely classic, *The Goshawk:* ". . . because the faculties exercised were those that throve among trees rather than houses, and because the whole thing was inexpressibly difficult." Absurdly, songwriter's words: cowboy singer Ian Tyson's, from his song about Charles M. Russell: "get 'er all down, before she goes." I turned back before I reached the river, climbed back into my bag, and slept fitfully 'til dawn. Later I read a passage in a travel book, Tobias Schneebaum's *Where the Spirits Dwell,* that suggested my agony was not unfamiliar: ". . .the wonder of being with new people who almost certainly had never seen an outsider for more than a few seconds at a time, the excitement of collecting successfully, all passed. What was I getting out of my time there? Information, somewhat meager, yes; photographs, yes. But that seemed to be all."

THE NEXT MORNING WE EMBARKED ON A LONG DRIVE SOUTH along the river, with its valley below us on the left and a steady progression of red cliffs and eroded rocks to our right. The mesa beneath us was marked on the map as a "road" but was unmarked by man; a flat plain of rounded pebbles two miles or so wide, too hard to take tracks. Critics of grazing in the west might be confounded by this desert . . . it has been overgrazed for millennia, I suppose, though no one seems to have known a different fauna here at any time in human history. The nomads' animals are fat, but at the expense of what? And what would you have them do? Only Stalin had the satanic hubris to force Kazakhs off their lands, and Kazakhstan, which he used as a prison colony, relocation camp, nuclear waste dump, atomic testing ground, biological warfare center, and who knows what else, is in worse shape than Mongolia. They even managed to dry up the Aral Sea on their eastern border.

Only two falcons disturbed the stillness of the plain. One, a rust-colored Eurasian kestrel, perched on a volcanic boulder and watched us go by, turning her head to acknowledge our passage, but not wasting any energy. The second, huge and pale tan, flew over our heads when we took a stretch at noon. At home I would have guessed it a rather off-color gyrfalcon; here it might have been one, or a saker. "Shunkar," said Canat.

Soon after lunch, what at first looked like a standing human appeared on the horizon. The plain was so flat and featureless we could see it from a mile away, the only break between the line of vegetation below the mesa's edge on our left and the palisades on our right. "It is a very good bulbul I told you about," said Canat. "Has carved head and face, features, not just rock." He also insisted that this one was a battle monument, not a tomb, though I thought the distinction might not be all that important after a thousand years.

We drove straight at it. It was carved of sandstone, perhaps five feet high, with a pointed beard, a cap, square shoulders, and two arms clasping a flask. Carruthers has suggested such monuments, which can be seen from Hungary to the Altai, are holding snuff bottles, still used by most Mongols. In fact, it looked a lot like some of the Kazakhs we knew. It was flattened, front to back, like a tombstone, and wore a veil of endless layers of white hawk droppings, the residue of a thousand years of being the tallest object in a plain ten miles wide by several hundred long.

Which offended Ed. Before Canat could even climb from the backseat, Ed was baptizing the bulbul with water from his canteen. Before I could ask him what he was doing he picked up a handful of dirty snow from the statue's protected side and began scrubbing. "What the *hell* are you doing?"

"Washing the bulbul. Americans don't like to see all this . . . shit." He was simultaneously kicking at some dried camel droppings.

"Wait a minute!"

Ed's arguments actually made sense in our world; it was just that I was beginning to wonder whether our worlds and the real one intersected at any point. He was probably right about the editors of glossy magazines and their consumers, fellow armchair romantics. Hadn't I been called to the Kazakh lands by an image? But by now I was on a reality binge. I argued that the droppings had been there for at least one, maybe two thousand years; that the only pictures of bulbuls I had ever seen, in *Nomads of Eurasia* and *Unknown Mongolia,* had been streaked with hawk chalk. Finally, I persuaded him to let me photograph the bulbul in all its maculate glory, while he moved the camel turds out of the frame. Doubtless he thought I was as crazy as I thought *he* was.

But the whitewash on the bulbul was a tougher task; we didn't have enough water in the Jip, never mind the canteen, to make a dent. After a few minutes he gave up, and we drove off the sharp edge of the plain down into the bumpy river bottom.

ARALBAI'S COLLECTION OF BUILDINGS, STONE PENS, GERS, and a house did not suggest a mere nomad's "winter-spending" place;

if I were to characterize it in American terms, I'd call it a ranch. But instead of white-faced Herefords and black baldies, we picked our way through fat-tailed sheep, stately black camels, and piebald yaks. A huge black-and-white herding dog with one blue eye came from behind the house to snarl at us, while a long-haired gray cat scooted under a disassembled ger. A pole beside the nearest pen, ten feet high, flew a startling, slightly sinister black-and-white pennant: a dead magpie hung by the neck, fluttering in the breeze.

An old man came out and spoke to Siassi. Canat said "Aralbai is in the hills hunting. This man will show us where." The old man climbed into the back, loosening his fox hat, and grinned through several missing teeth. We reversed, and bumped our way back up to the mesa.

This time we headed west, straight toward the rocks, until we were inside one of the sandy valleys that meandered through the surreal stone monuments. We drove up this one, then down another, seeing nothing moving at all. Only the occasional sheepherders' monuments suggested the hand of man. The landscape seemed as dead as Mars. Finally, on the third stop to glass the hills, Siassi noticed a white horse a half mile away. In minutes we were dismounting to shake hands with Aralbai.

I have a photo of him and his son Armanbek taken at that exact moment. The serious-faced ten-year-old holds one of the ubiquitous Russian .22 training rifles, and looks away from the camera. Aralbai himself is pulling off his enormous sheepskin gauntlet to shake hands. With his buzz cut, mustache, hand-rolled cigarette, and chaplike sheepskin pants, he looks as tough as the rocks; in fact, like the backcountry Kazakh cowboy that he is.

Canat had already told us that this was a man who, in Thomas McGuane's words, had "ruined his life for sport." He hunted all season with his eagle; shot game from birds to wild sheep with his .22;

and spent afternoons, when the ice was out, fishing in the river. And, in whatever spare time he had left, he ran one of the most prosperous "ranches" in the valley. Now he grinned and beckoned us toward a pile of rocks, on top of which perched his berkut. Unlike the other ones we had seen, she had the lean and hungry look. In fact, she was staring into the rock pile, feathers tight, head down, watching with the look of intent that only an aroused bird of prey can attain.

"Fox is in rocks. We must use stick and see if he flushes." Suiting his actions to Canat's words, Aralbai picked up an eight-foot pole and began to probe a crevice. For a while, nothing happened. The bird shifted her feet but did not relax. We probed hole after hole with no result. Except for the bird's excitement, I might have thought the whole charade was being played out for our benefit.

Until, as we were beginning to relax, the fox squirted out from under a boulder and headed for the next outcropping in an undulating tawny streak. The eagle had been looking toward Aralbai and missed the takeoff for a second, but she turned quickly at our shouts and thundered into the air, her great wings threshing for purchase as she climbed, then beating swiftly as she arrowed in on the fleeing dot. "It is *karsac,* small fox," announced Canat. For once, I didn't care about the animal's identity—I was just delighted because we were finally seeing some kind of action; in fact, I was laughing as we ran, despite the thin air and my heavy boots.

Atkinson, quoted in *Oriental and Western Siberia* said ". . . unless the animal can escape into holes in the rocks . . . death is its certain doom." When we achieved the rock pile, the eagle stood atop a round boulder half the size of a house, with a cleft below it deep enough to crawl into, pointing the cleft like a dog. The fox had disappeared.

Aralbai was not about to be bilked of his prey just because it was hidden in a jumble of rocks ranging from head and car size, to house size. He grabbed a handful of dried grass and stuffed it into the crack, as far in as he could reach, and lit fire to it. The old man climbed up to reclaim the eagle, lest she fly into the smoke. We began to circle around the fire, eyes on the bird, to probe other clefts; it was obvious that, in such a loose pile, the fox might be any-where, including already coming out of the other side. For a few minutes, Aralbai fed twigs to the flame, gesticulating and talking ex-citedly to Canat. "Aralbai say that if you come from America to see him catch fox, he *will* catch fox!" But nothing happened.

Then the boy raised his voice and pointed. Thirty feet from the fire, a tawny pointed head was assessing the situation. Before any of us could react he winked out like a light in the blackness of the lit-tle cave, as if deciding that five Kazakhs, two Americans, two horses, a rifle, and an eagle were not good odds.

Siassi, caught up in the excitement, pumped his fist in the air and made a loud bad-word noise. He climbed down and ran in the di-rection of the Jip. It was the first time I had ever seen him move so fast. He returned a moment later with a red five-gallon gasoline can and a length of rubber tubing, like the ones Suleiman used to give tea to the birds. I was so intent on the bird and fox that I didn't know what was going on until he climbed up onto the high rocks with the old man. To Aralbai's shouted encouragement, he used the tube as a siphon and began to sluice gas down into a hole about ten feet above where the fox had disappeared.

Even then I didn't quite get it. Once, in Florida, I had watched a redneck friend of a friend siphon gasoline into a gopher burrow so that the smell would chase out any rattlesnakes that might be lurk-ing in it. I didn't approve of it then and still don't, but it didn't amaze me that such practices would exist in the Mongolian back-country. Until Siassi followed the gas with a lit match, and flames shot up twenty feet into the air with a roar like that of a propane burner on a hot air balloon.

"Asshole!" I screamed at Siassi. He turned and smiled innocently. Immediately, I felt like a shit. My own desires had led me here, and now I was shouting at an employee whose only crime was that he was doing what he thought *I*—and Aralbai—wanted.

It was pretty stupid, though. Canat and Aralbai were shaking their heads. Probably the fire was nowhere near the fox in that aerated castle. But if it was, what good was a roasted fox to anyone? And if not, what better incentive to stay underground? After a few minutes the fire went out, leaving only a black smear on the rocks.

Somehow, though, ours had gone out too. Whatever anti-hunters may think, few sportsmen, even in so-called "primitive" cultures, practice deliberate cruelty, nor is there any pleasure gained from acting outside a formal pattern of rules. Aralbai, Armanbek, the old man, Canat, Ed, and I, hunters all, were embarrassed, ashamed, dejected, all at once. Only doggedly urban Siassi seemed blissfully unaware of the change in mood, whistling around his cigarette as he re-coiled his hose. His boozy "pragmatism" had ended our hunt for the day by turning it into a travesty. Nor could I ignore a deep feeling that it was mostly my fault. After all, I was the idiot who had traveled to the far side of the globe to see a bird catch a fox.

The sun was low over the hills now, turning them into black goblin cutouts. We headed back to the ranch for the inevitable feast. Streaks of red light lit up browsing camels with gold highlights and gave the yaks a fiery corona of backlit hair. The freshening breeze twirled the magpie on the pole, flying it like an evil kite. Even the outhouse, built precariously on thin legs out over the turd-strewn river ice, took on an unearthly glow. The black goats stared at us with reptilian eyes. It was a long way to Kansas, or even to New Mexico.

We wandered around in the waning light, taking it all in, while Siassi and Aralbai disappeared up the road in search of vodka. A rustle in the bushes resolved itself into an explosion of calling birds

when I pressed forward: Daurian partridges, not unlike our im-
ported "Hungarian" variety. A grazing yak ignored me as I circled it,
fascinated: *very* unlike a cow, with its short legs, round belly, and
horse's flowing tail. I gave two towering camels a wider berth; they
looked baleful and dangerous.

I brooded on the afternoon's acts, unable to get a handle on why
they bothered me so. Cruelty is distressing, but death inevitable; besides, the Kazakhs seemed to have a genuine affection for all animals, tame and domestic, despite Islam's reputation for caring only
for the human, and Allah. Perhaps their attitude toward their con-
geners is pre–Islamic; certainly it is deep. In my whole time in the
Kazakh country, I never saw a harsh word or blow fall on any animal.
Most households kept coddled indoor cats, even here in the outback. Dogs were spoken to in kind tones; horses were cosseted, petted, praised, and, always, fat. Even sheep were petted and
complimented. So I felt no disapproval for Kazakh practice; only a
too-easy irritation at Siassi. I finally decided that short time was driving me to perfectionism, a vice that blinds us all to the merely good,
and that I had inadvertently caused the bonfire in the cracks by
wanting too much, too soon.

When I walked back to the house, the party had begun. The table
was covered with little locally made vodka bottles, about the size of
American beer bottles, but with foil caps that could not be closed
after they had been opened; rather like the old cowboy game of
throwing away the cap on the Jack Daniels bottle. What's more, Siassi
told me with broad gestures that he and Aralbai had consumed *five*
on the way back.

The house was dark and virtually windowless, the scene lit by can-
dles. Packed around the table were Aralbai, his wife, his sister-in-law,
his seven children, our party, a cat, the eagle, and, in a fenced-off
corner, nine or ten very young lambs, inside to protect them against

freezing and wolves. I surrendered to the mood, tore the foil off the nearest vodka bottle, and toasted my host.

It was the beginning of a long, wet evening. The toast came back to me at once, and someone popped another bottle. We tried to talk a bit about eagle hunting, but it was hard to stay on track. Still, Aralbai, perhaps the most driven hunter we would visit, had a lot to say. He was properly fascinated with animal minds: "A dog will work for his owner; eagle works only for her food. A dog tries to know your soul." He solved for me the mystery of what Kazakhs do with their eagles during the molt, the long summer months when there is nothing to hunt. "We put her on a long leash, in a spot under the trees near the river. There must be beautiful things to watch, for her to see . . . she does not wear a hood. We get her fat. We feed marmot. We do not eat marmot ourselves . . . it has hands, like a human." He showed me the physical virtues of his eagle: "She has four stones" [large scales] "on each toe. This means she is strong." Finally he offered me a smoke, but the coarse Russian tobacco spilled on the floor and he replaced it with one he bummed from Siassi. His sister-in-law, a beautiful woman in her thirties, then demanded that Canat translate her compliment to me: she liked the way I looked when I smoked. While I blushed and everyone hooted, the next half liter began to make its rounds. As she drank her portion, straight from the bottle, I thought that Canat was right as usual. Allah might reign here, but there was no love for mullahs or Puritans. These women were tougher than most American men. Even in their traditional village roles, they could ride a horse all day, then come in and make bawdy jokes while drinking vodka with the men. And their daughters were learning to speak English and be doctors.

Aralbai asked Ed if he would like to film him feeding his eagle. He brought her to the table, where he held a bowl of washed meat in front of her on the table. Before he unhooded her, three of the younger children formed a human chain around the "animal babies" to protect them from the eagle's hungry eyes. When she finished, he pulled down a *domboro,* the Kazakh two-stringed guitar, and a child began to sing, shyly, eyes averted, a love ballad. Just as we were beginning to relax, Aralbai's wife brought in a two-foot platter heaped with steaming meat to the low table in front of me. The legendary, dreaded sheep's head had finally arrived; not just one, but two, plus a roll of horse sausage on the bone, a haunch of lamb and one of goat, a roast of beef, and a foot-high mound of sliced potatoes. Aralbai handed me a knife and a raw onion. But before I could say so much as "Bismillah," Ed—made bold perhaps by the unaccustomed amount of vodka—said "Let *me* do it!" He carefully cut a piece of meat from the sheep's lip, about half-an-inch-long, and extended it to Armanbek.

"Bigger!" whispered Siassi. Ed cut an inch-long piece, very slowly, and handed it to Aralbai.

"Stev! You do it. We're *hungry.*" I recaptured the knife and began to hack off chunks of fat. Everyone sighed and smiled. I felt properly accomplished, redeemed from our earlier folly.

The night slowly degenerated into a long series of toasts. I vaguely remembered that my last one had to do with an international exchange program for falconers. It had nothing on Siassi's, which began in Kazakh. After about two minutes I began to pick up familiar words in Russian . . . "horse . . . big . . . man . . . woman." I looked at Canat. "He is speaking very bad Russian. He is getting emotional."

Five minutes later he was still speaking, getting red in the face. Canat was giggling. "He is telling a whole fictional book. He is saying that Kazakhs used to live for a hundred year, more. He says it is because they had thirty young wifes. And ate raw horse meat." He waited, laughed again. *"Kazakh* horse only. He says it have different molecules."

Finally Siassi turned and toasted me in Russian. *"Nosdrovya."* I returned the salute, and we downed another glass. Two bottles later, Aralbai tumbled forward off his stool into the remains of the sheep, and his kids and his wife carried him off to bed.

I MANAGED TO SLEEP PRETTY WELL, DESPITE THE CONSTANT bleating of one of the "animal babies" (Canat's term). For once, I dozed until everyone else was ready to rise. Aralbai rolled out of his deep box bed with a groan, head in hands. But after a drink of hot tea and a home-rolled cigarette, he grinned, dragged over last night's platter, and pulled a sheep's skull from the congealed fat. He looked it over a minute, carved off a slice, then, remembering his manners, offered it to me on the point of his blade. I refused, I hoped not too quickly, took a bowl of tea from his wife, and crawled out to meet the day.

There was a high mist in the air, making the landscape look ancient and dead. Back home, such a morning would smell of impending storms.

I was pacing nervously, watching the kids reattach the animal babies to their mothers, when Aralbai came out to saddle his horse. The horse was a handsome little gelding about twelve hands high, white with pale spots, that resembled a Kazakh Appaloosa. "He says to tell you that if he has to ask all his relatives he will find you a fox," assured Canat.

But when we returned to the half-washed bulbul, we found that world views were about to clash again. Ed wanted to spend the day shooting Aralbai galloping romantically past the bulbul, combining the images of the dashing Kazakh warrior, the eagle, and the ancient monument. I—and, as far as I could understand, Aralbai—wanted to go hunting. Canat wanted us to come to a consensus. Siassi wanted to smoke and nurse his hangover.

Ed was entirely reasonable. "Look: no American magazine is going to run shots of an eagle ripping a fox apart. We could maybe get some action shots, but we can't rely on the fox to run our way. Our time is short, but if we get some good dramatic images, it'll pay our way back. Besides, this will just take a little time."

I looked at Canat. "If we leave today," he said, "we can get more supplies in Olgii. There is young eagle hunter in Altai who still has foxes, maybe wolf, deep snow. We can spend two days with him and you can still fly back."

Reluctantly, I gave in. The next four or five hours were an education in filmmaking. First, Ed had Aralbai gallop in endless circles around the bulbul. Then he had him approach the camera from a half mile or so away. The "image" was strikingly dramatic, a sort of *Lawrence of Arabia:* The Movie effect again. But it didn't show me anything other than that Kazakh eaglers looked splendid.

Next, Ed tried riding in parallel to Aralbai, holding his video camera. But something about the machine, or perhaps the clothes that didn't smell of sheep, put off the fierce little gelding, and he began to buck. Although Ed was a reasonably good horseman, the loss of a $2,000-plus video camera did not seem a sensible price to pay for a single shot.

Next, he hit upon a better way to film the galloping horse: to have Siassi drive parallel to the horse and rider, while he hung out the window toward them. This worked so well that he did it what seemed to be a dozen times.

He still wasn't getting exactly what he wanted. He had noticed that sometimes the hooded eagle would lose her grip on Aralbai's glove and then fly blindly at the end of her eighteen-inch jesses. As she was headed into the wind of their forward gallop she would maintain herself above the rider like an eight-foot-wide black kite. He asked Aralbai to ride toward him again, "flying" her this way. Then, to do it again.

I stepped in, trying to keep myself from a display of temper. "Ed. That's not falconry. That's eagle abuse. You're just getting her upset, and any falconer that sees that picture is going to accuse us of being fakes. Besides, it'll look so cool that every idiot art director in New York will want to use it instead of the *real* stuff."*

I wasn't sure I was getting through, but Aralbai called for a break to rest his eagle and his horse. I still have a photo of him seated on the stony plain, eagle and glove on the ground beside him, rifle slung on his back, rolling a smoke, as Ed, Siassi, and Canat confer in the background. As I snapped it he grinned, shook his head, and offered me a smoke.

If we left without going back to the ranch, we would have time to cover the treacherous back way to Bayaan Olgii before dark. Aralbai shook my hands fervently and said something to Canat: "Aralbai says that you should come back in the summer, to fish; and the fall, to shoot duck and fly eagle. He says if you will bring back American rifle, even old one, he will give you wolf, or snow leopard." I thanked him, and told him that I hoped to return; that I would find him a rifle; and that I did not need, and could not bring back, a snow leopard.

For me, the ride out, though more spectacular country than we had come through on the way in, was tinged with melancholy, as though it was the beginning of winter rather than of spring. The

---

* For the first published photo of our expedition, an art director picked a still from this series!

cold was fierce, and there was ice in the breeze. First we descended through a deep canyon, a dry riverbed with no tracks whatsoever, then emerged on the lee shore of a great lake. Across the lake towered the misty bulk of the forested mountains in Uvs, as dark and menacing as something out of Tolkien. Then we rode for hours under a wall of black cliffs, seeing only a single camel moving through the Martian waste. Finally we drove into the top of another canyon, briefly glimpsing buildings far below and miles away before we dropped into it.

This one was like a gigantic version of some riverbeds in the west. Its bottom was composed entirely of water-smoothed cobbles, from which emerged huge bare cottonwoods. We drove over rocks bigger than my head until, rounding a corner, we saw the oddest sight of all: a shining, black, brand-new Mercedes sedan with its trunk open, with a well-dressed man and woman in sable hat carrying armloads of bare branches to fill its interior. A half hour later we were back in Bayaan Olgii. It felt distinctly urban, despite its wood-hauling camels and ponies.

That night, refreshed by hot water and clean clothes, we went to dinner at the Disco Bar, where we promptly had our first and last Kazakh urban experience. Three huge young men in buzz cuts were at the bar, being young and loud. Siassi, dressed like something out of *Saturday Night Fever* in bellbottoms, thick-soled shoes, and a shirt opened halfway to his waist, caught their attention, and one began to jeer at him. He yelled back, and suddenly the biggest of all was leaning over the table, threatening him, and, apparently, us. He turned and poked a finger in my face, shouting.

I stood up, pushing back my chair for room, figuring that if we didn't say something we were going to be squashed like bugs. Canat put his hand across my chest, saying "No, Stev, wait, let me talk to him." He put an arm around the youth's shoulders and walked him toward the back of the room, smiling and speaking in a low voice. I looked over my shoulder to see Siassi all but running out the door, then back to Canat, who was returning with four beer mugs. Behind him came the former thug, who shook my hand western-style, and indicated that the beer was from him, for us.

"What happened?"

"They were just kids, from wrestling team. They thought you were Russian. Many here do not like Russians."

"But what did you say?"

"I told them that I did not know them, but maybe they know my name. I said, 'I am Canat, the soldier. If you are nice, I will buy you a beer. If you make fight, I will kill you.' They decided to buy *you* a beer, to apologize." They bought us two more rounds before we could leave, and toasted us as well, as though we were new-found friends.

The next day, totally out of money but for two large-denomination "Big Face" American bills in my money belt, we decided to go to the money lenders, who exchanged tugrugs at a better rate than the state banks did. The money changer's house held the strangest combination of objects I saw in Olgii. Naturally enough, a ravening Tibetan mastiff was chained at the gate, so furious at our existence that he bit down furiously twice on his iron chain. The decor, though, was just as odd, including a TV in every room, luxurious hand-stitched Kazakh wall hangings, the only cheesecake Arabic calendar I have ever seen, and a stethoscope hanging on the wall like a crucifix. I was eager to make our trip south, and relieved when the mastiff's snarls receded behind me.

Canat had been thinking about my questions and interests. Now he asked, tentatively: before we drove to the white wilderness of the high Altai, would we be interested in meeting his cousin, who lived nearby and was an eagle hunter? I had been asking about those who trained passage eagles, and his cousin was the one he knew who always did. Besides, he was a serious man, who thought a lot about important matters.

Manai, who owned no vehicle, lived thirteen miles out of town, in the Altai foothills. The next morning we drove out and up, and up and up—no river valleys here, only a vast uptilting plain. Finally we cut left and around a barren hill, curving ever upward, until we reached a bare valley at over 3,500 meters. A house and ger came into view on the hillside, both glowing white in the brilliant light.

It was the most desolate place I had ever seen for a house, and one of the most perfect. From where the lawn would have been, had there been any visible vegetation, you overlooked a little valley full of old snow, backed by an enormous bare brown hill that must have risen another thousand feet. Back the way we came, you could see the river valley where Olgii nestled, framed by desert crags. To the south, looming over the hills' shoulders, were snowy Himalayan peaks, looking impossibly high and sharp. Courting choughs soared and dived overhead, and flocks of tricolored hill pigeons soared in formation on the winds that blew eternally off the slopes. The scene was one that only a mystic or a hunter might love . . . or, perhaps, an eagle.

Behind the house was a striking tableau: a fat shaggy black horse, with a mane and tail that nearly reached the ground, and silver-studded tack; a hooded eagle on her tripod; and a trash can with two horse's leg bones, complete with hooves, protruding from its top. Behind them, a black volcanic outcropping, festooned with colorful laundry, was otherwise hard to distinguish from the stacks of blackened cow droppings the family used for fuel. What else, when you were thirteen miles from the nearest tree?

Inside, Manai and his fourteen-year-old son Kadan waited with their eagles as his wife prepared the feast. Manai had high cheekbones, a long jaw, large ears, green eyes, and a ready, gentle smile.

He wore a kepesh, a round Moslem skullcap, on his head. Later, Ed was to call him "handsome," which Canat would correct to "No, *strong* Kazakh face." What became apparent after a few questions was that here, at last, I had found my scholar-colleague.

Manai would only fly passage eagles, for their better flying ability and gentler virtues. He caught them in what western falconers call a "jealousy trap." He would take a male, or other less desirable eagle, and tether it next to a large carcass in a place where he had seen the eagle he wanted. The eagle would come in to evict the trespasser, and fly into a net stretched across. After that, he preferred to take less than a month until he flew the bird free at fox.

Training, he said to me, was simple, as I knew. He let them sit and fast for a week, hooded, then began training, feeding low-fat foods like sheep's lung and rabbit.

How long did he keep an eagle? No one should keep an eagle longer than ten or twelve years . . . they should be let go, to breed. His son's eagle was three, his two. The last eagle he had flown he had released at eleven. He put white cloth tags on her wing so he could recognize her. Now she was a mother; she had raised young last year.

Surely, up here in the hills, he had wolves. Was that not a young wolf's skin on his wall? Did he hunt wolves himself?

Wolves were dangerous quarry. Young men hunted wolves for glory. But it wasn't very safe for eagles. Had I heard about the hunter whose eagle had been killed by the snow leopard? Even foxes could be dangerous. His son's eagle was missing a toe on one foot, because she hit a fox on a slope, rolled, and momentarily lost her grip.

He looked at me gravely, and gestured to underline the importance of what he had said. Canat repeated it with the same cadence: "If you want to set your eagle free after ten years, *do not hunt wolves.*"

We shared photos and talked away the morning. He wanted to fly a falcon; could I send him a book? He didn't care much for male eagles ("Good for mice!" he joked) but they were useful for boys to learn on, and for catching females. He always molted his eagles un- hooded, in the river bottom, like Aralbai, but kept them hooded when around children in flight condition, because "when they are hungry, they are dangerous."

And, why, after everything, did he train eagles? First, originally, because it was a deep tradition. But second, for himself: because it was the most interesting thing he had ever known.

Canat said that both Manai and Kadan were famous balladeers. Would we like to hear them sing? Manai brought out his domboro and for the next hour we sat entranced as they played: martial- sounding horse-gallop songs; wistful love songs. Manai was good; young Kadan, already deep-voiced, even better. The Kazakh music sounded almost like Celtic ballads in an incomprehensible lan- guage; unlike many Islamic and Central Asian styles, it was more than accessible to western ears. I can still hum at least one of Kadan's songs now.

For the record, here are their subjects: Manai's first song was one of the sweet ones, about "human life"; his second was about eagles. Kadan's first, sounding more ferocious, was again about "human life"; his second, the sweet one I remember best, about wild birds; his third about "young woman, going to be wife."

Finally Manai rose, and apologized for being done with hunting for the season. He handed me a fox skin, formally, with both hands; then took down a hood from the rafters. This, he said, was an his- toric hood, very old, from his father's first eagle. He hoped I would honor him by accepting it. I should come back in the fall; he would even try to find a young wolf, if I needed to see that. I told him that I would come back, and that I would bring him an American hood.

He turned to Ed and said that he would be happy to fly the bird to the lure, even though he was not hunting again this year. His lure itself was fascinating: a whole hare carcass inside a marmot skin, with a fox tail tacked on behind. They went out to take the prettiest pictures yet. But I suspected I already had my best gifts.

I HAD DREADED NEWS OF BAD WEATHER, BUT OUR REAL obstacle came from another direction, entirely unexpected. We had known all along that we were on the brink of Tsagaan Sar, "White Moon," the Mongol fiesta to celebrate the start of the lunar year and the end of winter. A Peace Corps worker had referred to it as "National Drunkenness Week"; when I wondered aloud, at dinner with Kent Madin and one of his young American-educated Mongol crew, whether this was disrespectful, the kid had laughed out loud. "No way! I certainly wouldn't call me that week—I won't remember a thing."

Which had seemed funny, at the time. But now Canat's wife Aika returned from the airport with the news that all airline service to Ulaan Bataar would be suspended for ten days after tomorrow's last flight.

It was a disaster. Our tickets out of UB had us leaving in six days, and the Altai, even barring bad weather, would take at least three. But for nearly maxed-out credit cards, I was out of money; after I paid Canat and Siassi I would have less that one hundred dollars left. Our flying visit had shed its wing feathers. There was even a question as to whether we could board tomorrow's plane.

Our last day in Olgii was a weird mixture of sadness, celebration, and anxiety. I gave Canat a pair of binoculars, some Patagonia gear, and a sleeping pad he fancied. Since he needed a camera for his tour company, I offered to send him an old Pentax that had belonged to my late partner Betsy Huntington: he said he would be honored to accept it if I put "her name and dates" (birth and death) on the case. He gave me the boots and a wall hanging stitched in silk by his mother. I bought a sable hat for Libby from Aika. Siassi requested a bottle of "good American vodka"—Smirnoff!—from me, indignantly rejecting "cheap Russian no-good" Stolichnaya. Ed made a video of us all to bring to David, with Siassi raising the bottle to him in a maudlin toast "I lov you Daveed!" He then demanded my Russian bird guide, and, to my delight, made me write down a number of Kazakh names for birds. I had no idea that he was any kind of a naturalist, but he explained that his father had been, and the "next time" I should visit his native village down south, near China. Canat joked that he wanted my four-wheel-drive king-cab Ford pickup, which was in the "Kazakh house" photo. He called it "Huge Jip. I will give you camel, eagle, Shunkar, and two horse. Only catch: you must pay all shipping. Wouldn't you like camel in Magdalena?"

And a little mystery finally cleared itself up. A bit drunk myself, I asked Siassi why he would not say "Steev" rather than "Stev." He giggled: "Steev mean . . ." and ran his index finger rapidly in and out of a ring he made with his other index finger and thumb. Oh, great. *Now* I find out my name means "fuck" in Kazakh.

Finally, Canat shook my hands firmly, the Kazakh way, with both hands. "You come back, my friend. Bring Libby, bring Jackson. I have two camels, eight horses, many sheep. Come in fall, when trees are gold, weather is good. We will live in tents, and hunt with eagle, maybe shunkar. Best of all . . ." he grinned wider still ". . . we will bring *NO CAMERAS!* Well . . . *maybe* little point-and-shoot."

THE FLIGHT BACK WAS ANTICLIMACTIC IN EVERY WAY, AND one fact was almost heartbreaking: the French were aboard, and had actually seen a fox caught. My jealousy of them resurfaced to the point where I could hardly bear to speak; how dared they to live *my* dream? Ed had me disembark at Tsosentsengel again, to pretend I was on my way, face the camera, and lend some coherence to the narrative. I felt like a perfect ass as I recited.

Later I was to see myself reciting still another scripted shot, this one back at Manai's, as I hefted his eagle after they had flown it to the lure. I stare at the camera like a grinning fool and say: "This is my dream: to be in the Kazakh country with an eagle on my fist."

The writer James Hamilton Paterson has said more good things about the dubious connections between truth and video than anyone alive. Of the subject of a film about deep diving, he wrote in part: "Something happened to him which was entirely dependent on his being there and doing it, and what is brought back on film and tape bears the same relation to the event as the banalities of speech and writing might bear to a mystical experience. Certain things can only be lived, not eavesdropped." He is right, of course. But every word I said to the camera is also true.

BACK IN ULAAN BATAAR, WE HAD NEARLY A WEEK TO UNWIND. Choughs, ravens, and pigeons were courting and carrying things for their nests to niches in the facade of the old Lenin Museum. Days were longer, and the snow was almost gone. The kids were still playing hotel at the Bishrelt. Ed plunged back into society, while I scribbled, and brooded. I had to craft that article for *Men's Journal;* it was, after all, what was paying my way. I whiled away my time in the hotel, watching CNN and reading a Paul Theroux book that I had borrowed from the Peace Corps headquarters (the section on Mongolia was missing), and a French history of the Jesuits. The oddest moment came when I watched BBC coverage of the first "Countryside March" in England. For a moment I saw my friends' faces in Bayaan Olgii. How could I ever explain to them that these British people were coming to demonstrate before their freely elected government because it had decided to take away their right to hunt?

What I had wanted to see, I realized, was the real Bayaan Olgii, the real Kazakhs, as they were in this point in time, as they had become *now*. I wanted to see their symbiosis with their animals, and their newer one with machines. I wanted to see Kazakh falconry when it was still a way of life, not something "performed" for rich tourists. The first modern version of The Picture I had seen was the one with the camel, eagle, and solar still. It was still my favorite. I loved the way the Kazakh eaglers incorporated the modern—synthetic jesses, tires for perches—into their six-thousand-year-old tradition. It showed that this aspect of their culture was still alive, still evolving, not merely a dead ceremony.

I did believe that "real" existed, too, even in an age of deconstruction, and that I could tell it from that word I was beginning to loathe: "image." Yes, an image had led me here, but from the beginning I had wanted, however briefly, to live the life behind it. James Hamilton Paterson says, ". . . the camera cannot tell a lie but it some times cannot tell the truth for it sees neither with the eye of affection nor with that of knowledge."

In the line to check in at the airport a uniformed customs official passed up and down, carrying a bottle of vodka and a jade snuff bottle. I had been worried about the one from "Very Old" until I realized that he was *selling* his, and offering shots to anyone who talked to him, whether they bought or not. A line of "crusties," latter-day hippies with amazing dreadlocks who do not wash, recoiled in horror.

Beijing seemed petty and even more restrictive after Mongolia, the people hushed and deferential against the still-vivid memories of striding women and smiling men in UB. We ate the best Chinese meal of my life in the insulated compound of the Swiss Hôtel, with a young man standing beside the table whose only duty was to replenish the hot water in our tea, shooting it past our hands in a magical two-foot stream. The airport bar was off-limits, allowing access only to first-class, "important" people.

On the flight back to LA, I dozed, scenes from the outback playing in my head. One simple one recurred like a hallucinatory loop: watching one of Suleiman's eagles descend from where we sat above her on the stony ridge, black-and-white bow shape sweeping left, then right, over red Martian sands, diminishing until she pulled up with a final great flap of wings to the horseman's fist. In all my years of hawking I had never seen the hunter from a bird's perspective, and I knew I had a new version of the picture, moving, haunting, that would stay with me forever.

More importantly, I felt I somehow *needed* to see an eagle catch a fox. Maybe it was the French party's success that made the trip feel incomplete. I had sent a copy of my first draft of the article to a friend, Boston writer Monty Montgomery. Although he enjoyed it, he teased me unmercifully about, as he would say with audible quotation marks "achieving closure." "C'mon," he'd say on the phone, "admit it. You weren't philosophical about those Frenchmen. You wanted to *kill* them."

Well, not quite. But, apart from anything else, it gave me a clear, un-self-indulgent motive to go back. My book wasn't finished!*

---

* The article, finished, bought, and paid for, never ran. Along with several other pieces commissioned by Terry, it was rejected, *by marketing*, as too "odd." *O tempora, o mores!*

Canat and Kent got together to bring a group out for the millennial new year, almost two years after my visit, and it was a great success. I obtained some falconry equipment and other gear for Canat, and he let me know that expenses, if I returned, would be minimal. Moreover, the one person I had missed when over there, my wife Libby, wanted to go.

As the Germans say, with her I would steal horses. Also, I could coldly justify her presence even to a budget accountant: she's the more accomplished adventurer, the older Asia hand. Thirty years ago she and her late husband Harry Frishman were taking tour groups trekking in the Himalayas, when Everest Base Camp was still a two-week walk from Kathmandu. She is a former Outward Bound instructor who can ski, climb, ride, kayak, and cook professionally. Plus, unlike me, she is dauntingly cheerful and free of all neuroses. Finally, she's a better money manager than I'll ever be.

Canat, who was curious about my family, also wanted both Libby and Jackson to come, so I felt comfortably confirmed in what I wanted to do anyway. Jackson, in his last year at college, had to postpone, but Libby was, if possible, even more eager than I. This time we planned an October starting date, so that the eagles would be started but not jaded, and the weather a bit better.

Last, and best of all, a chance query on another subject to *Atlantic Monthly* magazine brought me into contact with its editor, Cullen Murphy. Shortly thereafter, he offered to pay my fare if I could add five hundred words to my already-written account, words about success; "closure." How could I hesitate? We booked a flight, through Korea this time, to save a day, and more than a few dollars, and asked Canat to book us a room at the Bishrelt.

PART 3

ℛeturn

C anat was putting in some time with a relief agency called F.I.R.E. (Flagstaff International Relief Effort), founded by David Edwards, in part because of the disastrous weather conditions and subsequent livestock die-off the year before, so we did not expect him at the airport in Ulaan Bataar.

Mongolia, in all its vastness, is in some ways like a small town. As they say in rural New Mexico, of the whole state outside the cities, if you don't actually know someone, you know somebody who does. I had already seen this in, as it were, print: two recent English-language travel books on Mongolia each featured people I knew. The first mentioned two biologists, one American and one Mongolian with whom I had been exchanging e-mail; the second, Aralbai! When I had last been in Ulaan Bataar, I had run into Kent in Fast Food, the restaurant complex across the street from our hotel. So it was no shock to be greeted with a casual, "Hey, man" by none other than Ariunbat, whom I had last seen three years before in my room at the Bishrelt, discussing whether to grow his hair long for a film. He explained that he was there to meet some other Americans coming in for F.I.R.E., but that his cousin Ariunbolor, who worked for Kent, was on her way to meet us.

I want to pay a special tribute to Ariunbolor, known to her friends as "Bobo." I have never known anyone who can do as much to make you feel at home, or to smooth out your problems. Words are inadequate to thank her for all she did for us on that trip, and continues to do as our Ulaan Bataar liaison now. In just minutes she cleared our baggage and bundled us into a truck for the trip to the Bishrelt. On the way, she also managed to defuse a road rage incident, when our driver inadvertently cut off two young toughs, and to get us in touch with Canat via cell phone.

Cell phones! Suddenly, every ambitious Mongolian had (at least) one. It seems that in the absence of phone directories everyone simply carries a phone or two and a list of current numbers. In Ulaan Bataar, and even in Olgii City, conversations are punctuated by bleeps and beeps and short musical phrases. Sometimes one phone will ring while its owner is talking on another. A little later, in one of Ulaan Bataar's new hot spots, we would be amused at the musical counterpoint provided by the ubiquitous phones as they competed with the background musical score.

But they weren't the only things that had changed in Ulaan Bataar. Canat had told us to meet him in the "Budweiser Bar" in the Fast Food complex. There was still light in the sky, so we walked up and down the street that led to the old State Department Store.

It had been utterly transformed. Lights! Ads in English! No fewer than three internet cafés in as many blocks. And, above all, *restaurants,* in more ethnicities than you might think would exist in the town: Chinese, German, French, and of course, Mongolian. It seemed that, in two years, Ulaan Bataar had become an international city, despite a lagging economy and the droughts and blizzards in the south that had brought in the relief agencies.

This became even more obvious when we entered the Budweiser Bar. I don't know what I expected exactly, but it was something down-market. Perhaps because of Siassi's love of Smirnoff, I had resigned myself to a place with a wall of "Bud" cans.

I could not have been more mistaken; the Budweiser was more upscale than anything available in Socorro County, New Mexico, where I live. All new construction of heavy polished wood, elegant tables, fine glassware on ceiling racks—and the beer was Czech Budweiser, one of the finest beers in the world, not the American piss-water variety with the same name. Appetizers included the distinctly Russian potatoes and caviar.

The city had likewise been transformed. I was to hear how drab it was, even after I returned home, by tourists who stayed in high rises near the airport and who didn't venture behind the facades of the Soviet-era buildings. Poor tourists! The whole city reminded me of the old apartment in Olgii City, that Arabian Nights jewel behind peeling concrete. Bright doors and odd advertisements provided only a hint of what lay behind them. We soon found not just one, but two, of the finest Chinese restaurants we had ever eaten in, plus French pastry shops, and nourishing "fast food," like milk tea with ground meat dumplings (an easily acquired taste in the autumn chill of northern Mongolia). The State Department Store now stocked a delicatessen full of sausages and cheese, and stacks of fresh fruit and vegetables. Even the Bishrelt's menu was rewritten and comprehensible, and Chicken Fantasy available, though sadly mundane.

Art and antique shops were everywhere. The money changers had gone out of business; the banks now charged little, and cash cards worked. Not that some surreal sight or incident wouldn't suddenly remind you that you were a long way from home. We never did get an explanation for the exceedingly peculiar clock outside the most modern, high-rise, glass-and-steel bank: it featured a bronze coelocanth atop a weathervane atop a sort of witch's hat, from which descended a circle of . . . *tentacles,* of different lengths, constructed of multicolored tiles. We called it the "Cthulhu Clock," after H. P. Lovecraft's monster of that name.

A few remnants of the old ways of business also lingered, though I doubt their ability to survive. We went to one deserted "Mongolian" restaurant that displayed a varied menu and beer and spirits list in the window, but whose actual stock reminded us of the old sketch on *Saturday Night Live* where, no matter what you ordered, you got a "cheeseburger." It soon became evident that the only entrée available was "soup"—broth of lamb with no meat—and that they had nothing to drink at all. Why they stayed open remains an utter mystery.

Perhaps the greatest contrast with the empty restaurant occupied a corner on the handsome street leading up to the embassies, a little north of Sukhbataar Square. La Capitale-Doula came to epitomize the "new" Ulaan Bataar for us. Named after the capital of Cameroon, its owner-proprietor is Claire Vizzo, a native of that country, who came to Ulaan Bataar with her American Peace Corps ex-husband. She liked it despite the cold. (The first time Libby and I ate there it was snowing on the passing Mercedes, trucks, horses, and cows, the last two of which looked odd in front of the pseudo–St. Petersburg facades.) She opened her restaurant with the help of a cook from Sierra Leone and two Mongolian waitresses dressed in colorful African cloth, and now served a delicious and original Afro-Parisian menu (chicken with cinnamon-hot pepper sauce, garlicky lamb, excellent pastries) complete with French wine for about a fifth of Santa Fe, or a tenth of New York, prices.

On our second day Canat took us to dinner with friends at still another annex of Fast Food, this a haut German restaurant with fine silver and linen, single-malt Scotches, and steaks that could actually be prepared rare. (For the record, not always easy to get in the rural west, never mind in a country whose staple meat is mutton.) Our hosts were a Mongolian businessman named Nyamdorj, and his elegantly dressed wife, Surenkhor. We had planned several days in the city to get over our jet lag (and to wait for a piece of our luggage that had ended up in Beijing to arrive on Korean Airlines), and they wanted to take us to their "country house" for a feast, showing us some of the sights of the hill and steppe country on the way.

A YOUNG AMERICAN WOMAN, A FIRST-TIME VISITOR TO Mongolia—she had come for a few days to work for F.I.R.E.—had asked Canat if she could accompany us. Canat agreed, though he seemed a bit reluctant.

We—Libby, me, Nyamdorj, Surenkhor, Canat, and Phoebe (not her real name)—drove east in Nyamdorj's gleaming white Mercedes sedan. This time, instead of a long black wool coat, silk tie, Hong Kong suit, and homburg, he was dressed casually in a fine cashmere sweater and trousers, as were his wife and Canat. In contrast, Phoebe was dressed in tattered jeans, running shoes, and a sweatshirt that reflected a hard week's work. Which might not have seemed odd except that she talked about once having tried to buy a ranch in our area of New Mexico, but deciding not to because "they" wouldn't let her put in her own airstrip. She also told us that she had taken the trip in part because she could write off the cost on her taxes, reminding me of my late father's injunction about how the rich stay that way. At least, unlike some other F.I.R.E. volunteers we met, she didn't ask us if the Mongolians were communists or if they used, as one American asked me, "European money."

I had never traveled in this direction from Ulaan Bataar. It took a long time, through quite heavy traffic, before the livestock became more numerous than the houses. To my amazement, we were on a paved highway, though sharp-edged potholes made it perhaps even more hazardous than the better dirt roads. We were traveling through immense brown-grass plains, edged to the north by a line of rounded hills shadowed on their northwest sides by stands of larch, naked as dead trees for the winter. To me it looked, but for the larch monoculture, more like Alberta, Canada, than, as Phoebe commented, the Navajo reservation.

We rolled on at some speed. To our right a jet swooped in for a landing, wheels down, then abruptly disappeared at the edge of a line of concrete buildings. Canat noticed me staring, and commented "Underground jet base. Was Russian." He went on to describe the line of bases on the Chinese border to the south, all empty, abandoned in the Russians' sudden exodus during the "Change. " It explained the odd buildings, devoid of even livestock trails, that Libby had seen on the flight in. He then told us of immense bases in Kazakhstan he had flown into when he was with the Russian army. I will not even attempt to describe these; one retired Ranger I trust was dubious about their very existence, but an ex-military intelligence friend seemed unsurprised.

But soon we were beyond all twentieth-century artifacts, as the hills got higher, the horses more numerous, and the road worse. We passed a walled cemetery, which Canat referred to as a "quiet town." Nyamdorj slowed and then left the road behind entirely, driving swiftly straight over the steppes. The noise and jouncing diminished immediately, and the car began to feel like a Mercedes again.

A half hour later we climbed a long, south-facing grass slope to-ward a cluster of gers tucked cozily under a hill. A string of ponies were tied to a horizontal rope, and sheep grazed the hillside.

The interior of the main ger was magnificent. Although it lacked the intricate wall hangings of the Kazakhs, its radiating support poles were painted in rings and concentric patterns like those in the eaves of a Buddhist temple. There were colorful rugs, and a television set. We were guided to stools and benches while a young man with a shaved head lit a fire in the stove. He was introduced as Nyamdorj's son, a monk-in-training, out in the country for a weekend with the family. Still warm from the car, I had entered without my coat, and noticing this, he brought me a felt jacket with braided trim on the cuffs and down the front. In five minutes, the jacket was unnecessary as the ger filled with heat and people.

Nyamdorj began to ladle a white liquid into bowls and passed them around—at last, the famous *airag*, the drink made from fermenting mare's milk. Most western descriptions libel it with nose-wrinkling comments like "sour" and "thin." While they are technically correct, yogurt is sour, and beer is thin—try to imagine good yogurt with the consistency of milk, a bit of carbonation, and a mild alcoholic aftertaste, and you'd be closer to the real (and delicious) thing. The alcohol content is so low that, unlike with the ubiquitous vodka, you can drink a lot of it. And it gets a lot better with food. Canat asked if we wanted to see a Mongol sheep butchering. I had previously seen one only in the movie *Close to Eden*. Kazakhs kill an animal conventionally and, being Moslems, must cut its throat. Mongols, perhaps because they are Buddhist or (more pragmatically) because they like to save the blood, have developed a more humane if startling method.

When we went outside the sheep was on its back, held lightly by four men, although it didn't seem to be struggling. As we watched in slightly uneasy fascination, one of them made a slit about four inches long just below its sternum, and then reached inside. Canat helpfully explained to Libby: "He will squeeze big pipe near heart and stop flow of blood until sheep dies." All remained still, without so much as a kick from the sheep, until its eyelids drooped and it relaxed. Five minutes later, its skin was off and its body was being dismembered.

Back inside the ger, one of the local women had produced a large galvanized milk can. As the chunks of sheep arrived they were layered into the can with bits of onion and garlic. Then one of the boys removed a glowing red rock from the dung-fired stove and put it on top of the meat. Steam hissed out in a puff. More layers of meat, spices, and rocks were added with a small amount of water until the can could hold no more and the ger was filled with clouds of steam. One of the cooks laid a rubber gasket, which appeared to be made from an inner tube, to the can's rim, pushed down the lid, and tied it shut with a rag.

They placed it on top of the stove to cook, and served us a cabbage and carrot salad, more airag, and cans of German beer while the ger filled with the delicious smell of cooking meat. No more than twenty minutes later, Nyamdorj lifted the can off the stove, opened it, and put the chunks of steaming meat into a large communal serving bowl.

Mongols and Kazakhs lead lives so similar in many respects, that teasing each other about small ethnic differences is one was of distinguishing themselves to others. Canat had always bragged about the more heavily spiced stewed meat of his people, and insinuated that the Mongol meat was rare, tough, and bland. But this pressure-cooked sheep was as tender as anything long-stewed, and I ate it ravenously, egged on by the young monk and his ever-present ladle of airag.

After the meal we sat back in the warm ger, replete. Nyamdorj produced the inevitable vodka and, through Canat, toasted us and all future ventures. Suernkhor told us, again through Canat, that she would make us coats like the one that I had just worn. Still again, I felt weirdly at home.

Then Phoebe, who had stepped outside, returned with a bulging sack, which I had seen her putting in the Mercedes's trunk when we were in Ulaan Bataar. She announced that she had brought presents, and decanted them onto the floor.

I felt acutely uncomfortable. F.I.R.E. provides donated second-hand clothes for Mongolians who have suffered in the last two years' droughts and storms; a laudable activity. We had dined earlier that week with Canat and an American ex-nun, who had together made a grueling trip into the hard-hit south Gobi, and the recollection of it brought tears to that tough woman's eyes.

But here on the floor of Nyamdorj's elegant ger was the detritus of our culture. Ripped and worn jeans—I have never yet seen a Mongolian citizen out at the knees—were entangled with oversized T-shirts emblazoned with various NFL logos, looking like the ones gang bangers wore back home. A hideous jointed plastic action figure with the physique of Schwarzenegger on steroids rolled to my foot.

Mongolians are a gracious people. Nyamdorj thanked her, and distributed some of the clothes to various children. I met Canat's eyes and he shook his head, a pained grin on his face. Libby surreptitiously grabbed the alien action figure and put it in her pack.

The awkwardness passed quickly enough as more drinks made the rounds. Nyamdorj invited us outside and offered us his horses to ride. Feeling full—and just a bit drunk—I declined, as did Libby. Phoebe accepted and mounted a stout little Appaloosa look-alike, with a flowing mane and tail. She was a good rider and galloped up-hill to join two teenaged boys already racing above. I basked in the sun, thinking not for the first time that, but for the Mercedes and the TV aerial, this could be almost any century; and that, curiously, I liked the contrasting details, if not quite as much as I liked the immense horizon to the south.

The return to UB was more eventful than the one out. Nyamdorj turned the car northwest and into the hills. When we came to our first river he just drove in, throwing up two rooster tails of water as he ground over the stony bottom. I was not used to seeing a Mercedes sedan used as an off-road vehicle, but the car seemed up to it.

We stopped once, where a slanting cave mouth cracked a stone face, a hundred feet above the road. We scrambled up into it, finding the roof blackened by a hundred fires. The floor was all rock and sloped at about thirty degrees, making one wonder where the cave's inhabitants had slept, or even built their fires. But it had once housed forty Buddhist monks who had fled Choibalsan's persecutions, spending the winter in the cave before being betrayed. Soldiers had killed them all. "When?" I asked Canat. "Nineteen-forties," he replied, his face for once without a smile. As we walked silently back to the car I wondered again what he might have seen.

The country became steeper and more forested as we rejoined a (normal, dirt) road. This was a National Park, said Canat, as we passed a cluster of gleaming white gers permanently installed under a red-rock cliff. In the foreground stood a forlorn, life-sized brontosaurus. These gers, with full modern conveniences, were apparently constructed for tourists. I told Canat I preferred the kind I already knew.

We had one more near-mishap. Crossing a second river, well past another camp, the Mercedes lost traction on the gravel of the far bank and spun its wheels. Momentarily, I had visions of a long walk. But, aided by shots of vodka and airag, we all piled out and shoved it up the bank by pure brute force. More toasts all around, and then on.

Just before we curved south again out of the hills I saw an incongruous sight. The river had been running parallel to us on our right, often masked by tall bare trees. As we rounded a last corner we saw a fly fisherman standing in the water, lit by the reddening late afternoon sun. His rod curved back to throw a line of glistening golden drops, then forward, with perfect grace, to fall lightly on the water. He was wearing a cowboy hat, and looked as though he were in Montana—or, maybe, *A River Runs Through It.*

Ulaan Bataar, topped by clouds of orange dust, was a truly red city in the sunset. From the warm leather seat of the car, it seemed huge and remote and just a bit sinister in the dusk. Sated, sleepy, moved all at once, I recalled familiar Kipling lines: ". . . dreamers dreaming greatly in the man-stifled town; / We yearned beyond the skyline where the strange roads go down."

Quietly I asked Phoebe why she would think that someone who owned a Mercedes and forty horses would need secondhand T-shirts. Her answer was unrefutable in its terms. "But of course they're poor. They live in *tents.*"

OUR FLIGHT TO OLGII ON MIAT WAS A BIT TAMER THAN ON MY previous visit. We saw neither guns nor sheep nor gasoline cans, although the attitude toward carry-on baggage was still far more liberal than in the west. We arrived without incident to be met by Canat's wife, Aika, now the co-director of Kaztour, their ecotour company, and Bolatbek, a young, skinny Kazakh, who looked barely out of his teens. Canat was to join us when he finished up his F.I.R.E. business in a few days.

Aika's English, while improving, was still uncertain. Bolatbek's, though, was astonishing; he sounded like an American college student. "Let me get you guys' stuff in the truck—it's, like, too cold to stand around." Bags packed into Canat's big green transport van, we listened as Bolatbek introduced himself. He was an English teacher, as was his wife. He was three years out of college, and had a two-year-old daughter. He was hoping that working as a translator for Canat would lead to possibilities with tour companies. Could we help him with applications? What postgraduate courses were offered in American colleges? Did we think *A Tale of Two Cities* was a good book?

Akbek, the driver, was even younger. The crew exhibited the amazing physical diversity of the Kazakhs, who stand at an ancient crossroads of Asian and "European" peoples. Aika looked almost Mediterranean; Bolatbek rather Chinese with straight black hair, Asian eyes, and an aquiline nose; while Akbek, slightly Asiatic (but green) eyes, was redheaded, freckled, and, with his baseball cap, looked like an urban Irish kid from Boston.

I was exhausted; jet lag had finally caught up to me. When we entered Canat's new guest apartment, a crew, including Canat's urbane, Turkish-looking sister, was still putting on the finishing touches of a redecorating project. As always, it looked wonderful inside, though we had been greeted by a cow standing in the dumpster outside the door when we drove up. Even inside, it was chilly. Olgii City, like Ulaan Bataar, is heated by a central system. Not only was Canat's apartment further from the steam plant than the one from my first visit, but it was only October. The apartment blocks heat up gradually. At least we were on the ground floor; I understood that the top floor could *really* get cold.

None of which seemed to matter much. Our luggage exploded into the room, and we augmented the bed with our sleeping bags.

Aika was bustling around the small woodstove in the kitchen, while Bolatbek kept up a storm of questions. I just wanted to sleep. Somehow we managed to wolf down an enormous pile of spicy sheep and rice, and I went straight to bed.

I was awakened about two A.M. by a spasm of racking coughs. I could barely get my breath, and felt feverish. It seems stress, exhaustion, coal smoke, and dung-enhanced dust, not to mention the ten degrees Fahrenheit outside temperature, had done in my always-temperamental lungs. I had a sharp pain in my chest that stabbed through me every time I coughed, and I could not stop coughing. Despite my fever and exhaustion I was a bit scared. By reason of a trick of my physiology I am more prone to pneumonia than anyone I know. And no matter how heedless I tend to be, I doubted that Bayaan Olgii was the best place to come down with it. Besides, I was something past eager to go hunting.

Libby fed me gallons of tea at dawn, and I checked the bathroom to find that from seven to seven-thirty, there was enough hot water for a bath. There was no plug for the tub, but Libby pressed a potato wrapped in a plastic bag into service. I rubbed down in the chill air, dressed in my warmest clothes and huddled on the bed with another cup of tea (this one spiked with vodka) to await the arrival of Aika and Bolatbek.

They bustled in at ten, which seems to be about the earliest that any Mongolian citizen I know finishes their family obligations and goes out. Aika was concerned, but in control. *"Doctor* Aika," she said grinning, and indicated to Bolatbek to explain.

"She says all Kazakh women are doctors, because they have to be. They have some school training, and some traditional medicine."

She did indeed. She instructed me to take the antibiotics from my kit, while she sat a great pot of water to boil on the woodstove. First, she poured the boiling water into a large galvanized pan that she placed on the floor by my bed. "Put your feet in," she said, as she stirred in a yellow mustard powder. I did. It was *hot*. I yowled and attempted to back up, but she insisted. "Hot is good!" Somehow, I managed to keep them in, hovering above the bottom, pulling them out and dipping them back in again, cursing. Libby was in hysterics.

Next came the inhalation treatment. With my feet still in the now-tolerable basin, I was given another pan, this one full of herbs and what seemed to be crushed aspirin, to breathe. Aika smothered my head, upper body and the pan with sweaters, and topped the whole thing with Libby's storm jacket. Between my hot feet and the sauna atmosphere around my head, I was not only suffocating; I was sweating through my clothes. Aika insisted that I stay under for fifteen minutes. When I emerged I was breathing more easily, if only in contrast. "Now stay warm!!"

Aika repeated the treatment three times that day while keeping me full of tea and (fully dressed) under the covers. In the evening she called in a Kazakh woman who, though she wore a traditional head scarf, seemed to be a genuine house call-making MD. She examined me with a stethoscope, thumped my chest, and put an ear to it, before launching into a long explanation to Aika. "She says you have pneumonie-bacteria. She say you must take antibiotic." She looked at mine and shook her head, then wrote something in Russian on a page of lined paper from my notebook. Aika handed it to Bolatbek, who left to fill it with no further ado. Though as far as we could see only bootleg vodka shops were open past five P.M., he seemed to know exactly where to get antibiotics, not to mention the other remedies she had ordered: something called "Dr. Mom," in English, and rubbing alcohol.

"Tomorrow, special medicine," announced Aika as she left. I fell asleep feeling at least relaxed, if still anxious about getting out.

I woke feeling refreshed. Soon after, Aika briskly entered carry-ing a plastic bag full of steaks. "Horse meat," she said, and began to cover them with ground pepper. "Special medicine" was apparently going to be horse pepper steak. As I hadn't eaten much the day be-fore, this seemed like an excellent idea.

Until she took the steaks, put them in a pan of hot black tea, and told me to go back to bed and take my shirt off. As I sat there in dis-belief she enlisted Libby to help bind the warm steaks around my chest, covering them with, first a green plastic trash bag, and second, bath towels. She lashed everything down tight with a piece of torn sheet, and told me to put a sweater on over it all. "How long do I wear this?" I asked with a note of rising panic.

"Twelve hours."

Wearing the steaks around the house was no problem, although I did feel like the Michelin Man; Aika had anchored them so they were as tight as a wet suit. Although the apartment was on the low edge of cool, I was sweating as though I were in the tropics. I con-tinued to drink tea and stare at the intermittent line of camels, mo-torcycles, and Jeeps passing in the dusty street, and the already snow-edged mountains above them, where I wanted to be. At least I was no longer coughing.

Bolatbek came over to quiz us about life as a student in America and tell us about its equivalent in Mongolia, as well as about his work. I was propped up on the headboard of the bed, wrapped in meat and wool, while Libby sat near the foot; "Boka," as he preferred to be called, stretched out with his head over my legs and his feet on Libby's with the ease and physical unselfconsciousness of a well-bred pup. He spoke of the strict standards of English where he and his wife, the only ethnic Kazakhs there, had studied in Hovd; of home-sickness, and how bad the mosquitoes were there. He told us how hard it was to get books on a salary of $125 a month, and asked if we

could get him some English books. He exclaimed over the illustrations in my Russian bird guide: "Cool!"

Then he asked us to dinner. I looked at Libby, knowing she was
worried about my lungs. "Just keep the meat on!" she said, echoed
by Boka, who seemed in awe of Aika. I agreed, but I begged them to
wait until eight o'clock, which was a bit late by Olgii standards. Not
only did Boka have a dog; I was determined never to go to a social
engagement wearing meat.

I PEELED OFF THE WARM—NOW CLAMMY—SODDEN STEAKS AT
seven; a little early. I felt surprisingly good. Bolatbek lived in a walled
compound with his extended family, a big black dog, some sheep,
and a flock of red and black chickens. He, his wife Acemgul, and his
two-year-old daughter Akhmaral ("White Deer") had their own sep-
arate little adobe house within it. Like most "modern" Kazakh
houses it was much warmer than most apartments. First, it was small,
low, and built with thick walls of logs and mud bricks. Most importantly, though, it incorporated what some Americans call a "Russian
stove"—a hollow brick wall with baffles somewhere near the center
of the house, with an iron stove venting into it low in the wall. The
result was a thick white wall that radiated heat on both sides, from
top to bottom. Considering that in the towns you also had electric-
ity, and even running water—flush toilets, granted, are still rare—
and you could see why Canat and Bolatbek both preferred such
houses to apartments. Besides, all the new western-style buildings in
town were draining off even more steam, taxing the central heating
even further.

The evening passed warmly, and quickly. The toasts that often prolonged social occasions were absent. Bolatbek and Acemgul were apparently practicing Moslems, and their other guest, Craig, was a teetotaling American Christian who nevertheless was full of cheer, bantering with Acemgul about hoping to marry a Kazakh woman, and telling us that we should return next year to catch the second "Eagle Festival," when most of the eaglers in Bayaan Olgii Aimag gathered to fly their eagles, show their wares, and compete for prizes.

This gave Bolatbek an idea. Canat wasn't coming until two days later, and I was eager to see hunting. He had an old uncle in a village nearby who had won prizes at the first festival and, what's more, caught a fox on the way home. Should we visit him?

"Early"—ten-thirty—the next morning, Aika assigned us the green van and the services of Akbek. Over the last two trips I had become accustomed to the idea that starting times were provisional: the hour when you first met, but before you transported relatives, picked up extra passengers, and stocked up at the market. This time was no exception. First, at Bolatbek's, he went inside for a long time and returned accompanied by Acemgul, dressed in high-heeled boots and city finery. "My husband is *very* angry!" she said with a grin, though he looked more sheepish than angry to me. When we welcomed her, he relaxed enough to direct Akbek to the next stop, where we picked up two young boys and a girl. Apparently, when they were not in school in Olgii, they lived in the village we were visiting. One had come to Olgii on a motorcycle and this was his first trip in an enclosed vehicle. Everyone piled onto the benches that ran along the sides, while I sat in beside Akbek in front.

We drove north for ten or twelve miles in a straight line over no clear road, low hills rising to the west. Boka was in his element, pointing out hills, camels, and trucks with equal enthusiasm.

Although he was a dedicated teacher, guiding did for him what traveling did for us: brought him into contact with new people and ideas and, he hoped eventually, lucky places. He wore a flat, black polarfleece cap with a brim that I had given him, knee-high Russian cavalry boots, and a white athletic jacket, which made him look younger than his elegant wife in her sophisticated garb. Akbek, whom we had privately named "O'Leary," still looked like a Boston Irishman or, rather, teenager.

Perspectives in Mongolia seem bigger and longer than even those in the American west. The plain we traversed was as barren as anything I had ever seen: iron-hard bare dirt; tire tracks, rocks, and assorted dung; miles wide. It was as though all the tracks from the north of Bayaan Olgii and Siberia converged here to run south to the city, carrying all the traffic and all the grazing animals.

We saw the little black hill on the left, miles to the northwest, for what seemed like an hour before we finally reached it. It stood in front of the wall of hills that lined our plain to the west. When we drove behind it to begin our ascent to the plateau above, the grass reappeared, even as the vistas stretched out in still-greater splendor and size. The hazy sky of the valley broke up into alternating bands of blue sky and gold light, then turned black as thunder, then opened up again. Great walls of granite seemed to block our path in the distance, then fall to one side or another as we dropped into deep canyons.

Every minor ridge we crested led our eyes toward taller mountains, deeper valleys, gold fields in which grazed herds of black camels, cashmere goats, sheep, and yaks. We came upon a family heading down toward their winter pasture, with a riding camel and a horse leading, followed by two fully laden camels carrying their ger and its frame on their backs. Another family, dressed for the city in fine furs and wools, entirely covered a motorcycle and its sidecar.

We stopped once in the middle of a drove of sheep to ask directions from its mounted herdsman. We stopped again so that the boy experiencing his first car ride, which he was not liking, could be sick.

Bolatbek had said that his uncle's village was "very near, about twenty-five kilometers." By now we had been driving at a good speed for about two hours and had seen nothing but rocks and hills, flocks and nomads. The country was too magnificent to become bored, but we were still relieved when we descended a final canyon to see in the distance a wall of snowy mountains across a vast green river bottom, and the relief of homecoming on everyone's face. Even the carsick boy started pointing and chattering.

As we emerged into the river valley the walls of the canyon fell away. The river, an upper arm of the Hovdsgol, ran from north to south in endless unchanneled arcs and oxbows, lush and green even in the cold October light. The mountains across the river were the highest we had seen yet, bare and blue and forbidding, marbled with glaciers and peaks of shining white: the high Altai range, with Siberia, China, and the highest peak in Mongolia all less than fifty miles away. On our side of the river was a long sloping plain of black volcanic rock, sparsely interspersed with stubble and topped by sculptured cliffs of eroded rock. All through the valley yaks and camels grazed. As Libby said, it looked like a meeting of western Montana and Death Valley in the Arctic Pleistocene.

The tiny village of Ulaan Huus—"Red Birch," after the trees that lined the stream—was still about twelve miles to the south. We did not pause there, but continued south until we arrived at a cluster of neatly finished stone and adobe buildings and log corrals perched high on a sandy bank above an oxbow: the compound of Bolatbek's relatives. Acemgul covered her city finery with a shawl and a Moslem-style scarf over her hair, "for respect," and we parked the car beside two tethered camels and a saddled horse.

The welcome was warm even for rural Mongolia. Bolatbek's uncle, aunt, several younger couples of various cousins, and at least a dozen children swarmed around us as we were invited inside for the usual sheep-centered refreshments. But there were more treats than we were used to—fresh yogurt, perhaps the best I have ever tasted, mild mozzarella-like soft cheese, and fresh noodle soup in addition to the usual mutton bread, frybread, and white and orange hard curd. Our milk tea was laced with thick, sweet fresh cream.

Next we were led out for what was obviously a well-planned round of activities. First, Bolatbek and his uncle, a tall, Asian-looking Kazakh with a permanent grin and a Kirghiz hat like a white-felt inverted flowerpot, galloped on their horses to round up a female camel for milking. As they chivvied it toward the buildings, whooping like cowboys, a peculiar and very loud noise, a combination of a roar, a fart, and a grinding engine, issued from behind the buildings. "Baby camel," said Acemgul, gesturing. The spindly, sweet-faced infant blinked its long-lashed eyes at us and emitted the incongruous sound again—as Libby said, a very odd sound indeed for such a dignified mammal. The camel's milk was sweet and rich, almost as though it contained honey.

Then came a photo session. First, we were perched on camels for a quick ride around the compound. The hardest parts are at the beginning and the end of the ride, because of the rocking motion the beasts make when kneeling to allow you to get on and off; *riding* a two-humped camel is ridiculously comfortable, like driving a sofa with airbags fore and aft. Then we took about ten rolls of film of everybody, in every possible combination. One ten-year-old, wearing a Reebok sweat shirt (and so, of course, inevitably dubbed "Reebok") insisted on being in every photo with every being, unless forcibly removed; he even managed to insert himself into a shot of moldering camel skulls on the roof.

Finally, Bolatbek led me to the house of his great uncle, the eagler Khairatkhan. Khairatkhan was in his seventies, with a fierce mustache and a nose like an eagle's beak. He was the only man left there
who still dressed in traditional Kazakh eagle hunter garb: long corduroy coat cinched in with a silver-studded belt, twenty-six-fox hat,
high boots. He was obviously in pain from a bad leg and hip, and at
first seemed a bit dour and suspicious. He warmed a bit after I recognized an eagle-hood pattern hanging from a hook; perhaps I was
a falconer after all. But he dashed my hopes of seeing a real hunt
that day; his hip hurt too much, and the foxes were too far away. I
gave him a pair of binoculars, which he accepted without a smile.

He did want to fly his bird for us, though. He led us to the edge
of a courtyard where she was tethered to what looked like an old
rusty anvil, and cautioned us not to get too close. She was a first-year
bird with a white tail base and a bad attitude; she bristled aggres-
sively and raised her crest as we studied her. For the first time, I
thought, I was seeing the dangerous eagle of legend. Unintimidated,
Khairatkhan edged her onto his gauntlet and popped the hood on
her head. Outside, he went to get his horse. "Let's ride," said Bolatbek. We mounted the horses that he and his uncle had used to fetch
the camel, and galloped toward a ridge on the west side of the valley, laughing and racing over the black stones.

Everyone else converged on the ridge. Akbek and Libby had
loaded the horde of kids into the car. Khairatkhan left the fox skin
lure below with one of his sons, and trotted up toward us, eagle on
his right fist, with a more dignified speed than we had displayed.
When he reached us, he dismounted and unhooded the eagle.
Down below, his son started dragging the lure behind the horse,
bouncing it along the rocky plain.

This eagle showed none of the mild manners of Suleiman's or
even Aralbai's. She slammed into the lure as though she meant to

rend it apart. Khairatkhan made her fight for it, as some of the Kazakh eaglers had done in the Russian film, until she was panting and furious, talons buried in the pelt, crest up in a circle around her blazing eyes. If a fox had appeared on the ride back I think she would have pulled Khairatkhan's arm off trying to get at it.

Back home, mellow after his bird's satisfyingly ferocious display, Khairatkhan gestured to Bolatbek, who brought out a carved birch arm support, a set of jesses, and a beautifully embroidered gold-on-blue hawking bag. "He wants you to have these . . . the bag took first prize in the eagle festival." I accepted them gravely, and asked if he was training the son who had held the eagle to carry on in his tradition. Khairatkhan shook his head and laughed. "He says no! If his son hunts with eagles he will neglect his family and his animals. He says that hunting with eagles is an addiction like drugs, like vodka." He laughed again, and I realized that he considered himself lost, and had no regrets whatsoever.

GOING BACK TO THE VAN, WE FOUND EVERYONE LAUGHING hysterically. Most of the back of the van was occupied by four-foot-high woven plastic sacks, from one of which protruded the indignant horned head of a live sheep. Between gasps, Libby explained that five of the sacks contained dried dung for Boka's stove. The sheep, a future meal, was going there as well, but she had not submitted willingly. Apparently on first being "bagged," she had poked her hooves through the flimsy material and gone scrambling and sliding through the van's interior, scattering handlers, dung, and bags alike. Finally, after escaping the van entirely, she had been captured again and *double*-bagged. She remained quiet for the ride back to Olgii, though her photo does not reveal if she was exhausted, philosophical, resigned, or plotting her future escape. It may say something about our acclimatization that, until Canat lectured Bolatbek later on the inadvisability of taking on freight without asking permission, we had seen absolutely nothing odd about sharing our ride with a sheep and five sacks of dung.

BACK AT THE APARTMENT IN OLGII, WE WERE GREETED BY CANAT, still in his city clothes. Over mounds of spiced mutton and rice, bottles of Russian beer, and shots of vodka, we discussed our plans. At this point, we really *needed* to see an actual, successful fox hunt. I asked about Suleiman, but Canat said that he had died recently of a heart attack, leaving Aralbai and Manai as our two most active "familiar" hunters. Suleiman was a real loss. His merriness, showmanship, and sense of humor had been the best possible introduction to the eagle people. I wished we had been able to go on a real hunt with him; he would have choreographed it like a dance, complete with music.

Aralbai, the man "who ruined his life for sport," was certainly a possibility. Canat had already involved him in his "custom Kaztours." He told us that he had been approached by a Japanese businessman who had wanted a one-man trip that would include his two favorite activities: fishing and drinking. He wanted to go to Mongolia for its cheap vodka as much as for its monster *taimen* (a great carnivorous trout that eats muskrats and ducks). Canat picked him up at the Olgii airport, filled the truck with cases of generic foil-capped vodka at about $4 American a bottle, and drove east for five hours until he reached Aralbai's summer camp, where Aralbai reclined on the river bank with a long pole and a bottle. He dropped off the client and returned to pick him up ten days later. All the bottles were empty, and the client added a two-hundred-dollar tip, saying he had never in his life had such a fine trip.

But there were other advantages to Manai. He lived relatively nearby, so we needn't camp out or strain his facilities. He was, if not as good a drinking companion as Aralbai, a more serious man, in the sense of the French term *un homme sérieux*. And, technically, he flew the more difficult yet more accomplished, better-mannered "passage" birds. We agreed, given the shortening time, to concentrate on Manai and the near Altai range south of town.

At ten-thirty the next morning we answered the knock on the door, to be greeted by a grinning Canat saying "Look who I found!" He stepped aside to reveal a shyly smiling face of none other than Manai, who took my hand in both of his. He seemed moved almost to tears. "He is glad you came back. I think he did not believe you really would!" When he let go my hands, he reached into his pocket and came up with a homemade pouch, which held the binoculars I had given him on the first trip. He bowed his head. Waving a finger, I plunged into my luggage and came up with a falcon hood by Oregon hoodmaker Bryant Tarr that I had ordered in Islamic dark green, fitted for the saker or "shunkar" that I knew he wanted to train. Once again he grabbed my hands and poured out his thanks, as I vowed I *must* learn more Kazakh.

Manai had come into town to visit the market on his motorcycle. We agreed to follow him back that afternoon for sheep and tea; his boys were out hunting at the moment, but we could go out tomorrow. I couldn't help recalling Canat's warning on the previous trip about the effect of motorcycle-driven drafts on teeth; Manai seemed to be missing two since I had seen him last.

The road climbed to the south just as I remembered. There was more grass than I had seen last time—this part of Mongolia had been spared the worst of the droughts. The braided brown roads still stretched two miles wide across the high valley's bottom, heading south toward the pass that led into the Gobi Altai and, eventually, east toward Ulaan Bataar. We stopped at the crest to look back into Olgii, clustered below us along the Hovdsgol; the ground at the "rest stop" was covered with a hundred severed sheep's feet. We continued south over a pass toward a frozen blue lake that filled a depression at, perhaps, nine thousand feet above sea level. Bare mountains with burnt-black, crusted edges, dusted with snow like confectioner's sugar, receded endlessly on both sides toward still higher white peaks with sharp-edged planes like those in the late painting of Karl Rungius, abstract shapes that looked—almost—constructed. The usual camels and yaks grazed on the yellow grass slopes.

We turned left eventually and climbed the final slope to Manai's cold freehold, his motorcycle puttering on ahead. The same choughs and hill pigeons wheeled overhead. A fox skin and a fresh wolfskin dangled from the house beams. I ducked in out of the cold. Manai put away his supplies and asked for food to be brought, then disappeared behind a curtain. He returned wearing his kepesh, the ornate indoor hat worn by Turkic men, and holding the hood I had given him. He explained through Canat that I must take a picture of him with it, both so I would remember him, and so that Bryant would know how much his hood was appreciated.

Halfway through the meal something caught his eye and he gestured for us to come to the window. He could see his sons returning. We went over and, with the aid of our binoculars, spotted two horsemen about a mile away on the bare hillside, as small and slow-moving as ants on ice cream. We knew they would be awhile, and returned to the familiar warmth of tea, sheep, and the dung fire.

When we heard the jingle of the horses in the courtyard we were in the middle of the feast, but Libby couldn't resist going out. The eagle was a huge passage bird, the largest I had yet seen, and of an unusually pale chocolate color. Having seen Manai's birds before, I expected her to be easygoing, but Libby was amazed. The two boys, ten and (holding the bird) eleven, dismounted and greeted the stranger; then the one handling the bird tossed her to the ground, unhooded. Libby wrote in her notes: "Steve had told me how nice they are but I was still amazed when the boy stroked her head, like we would a dog, *unhooded,* and then picked up one of her feet to get her to his glove. She hooded up without a flinch or a duck." When they came in, Canat told us that they had seen and flown at a small wolf, but missed.

Manai wanted us to make arrangements with another eagler across the "road" to join us on the hunt the following day. We descended to the plain and headed toward a house about five miles away at the foot of the hills.

Libby again: "We had to cross about a hundred 'roads' at ninety degrees to get there. Canat made it a bit like a slalom course, running across them at an angle because the ruts are so deep. At the bottom of the volcanic hill on the other side we saw a bunch of upright stones, maybe fifty, which Canat told us marked graves; also a big mound, marked with a square of stones, big ones at the corners and small rings outside . . . a burial mound. Canat said that soldiers, coming through the passes, each would place a stone in a mound on the way to battle. On their return each survivor would take a stone away and they could tell how many had been killed."*

The inhabitant of the house above, tucked cozily into the volcanic rocks, with two camels tethered like sentinels on either side of

---

* The complex of stones here, south of Olgii, is virtually identical to one described by Douglas Carruthers in his 1913 *Unknown Mongolia*, up in the Russian Altai to the north; it is pictured in volume 1, across from page 66: "Tumulus and Monuments on the Chulim Steppe."

the gate, agreed to meet us with his eagle, and we turned back toward town. The late-afternoon sun had turned everything pale blue and gold, snow shadow and grass, like a conventional Mongol watercolor. I had thought these idealized before, but at this time and season, they were utterly realistic.

We drove into the hills the next morning with a rising sense of anticipation. Canat said that we would climb up onto the still higher plateau on the west side of the road and pick out a vantage point from which we should be able to see Manai, his apprentice, the eagler with the camels, and his older son, Kadan. The truck ground up through a narrow pass to emerge into the bleakest landscape I had yet seen. Snow covered the grass, and the only contrast was provided by black volcanic rock and the far-off pepperings of sheep, goats, camels, yaks, and horses.

We drove through a great silence. Whenever we stopped and turned off the engine, the only sounds were the pinging of the engine and the hiss of a breath of wind blowing ice crystals across the dry rocks. We climbed to the top of the hills and glassed the endless roadless uplands below. In a hundred square miles there were no visible traces of humans, at least at first. Canat guided my eyes until I could see, miles apart, stony "winter-spending places" carved into the sides of peaks like Tibetan fortresses. Every hour or so we would see a moving horseman or two, but, when we brought them into focus, we'd see only the rider, the horse, the flowing cloak of untrimmed tail; never the unbalanced, two-headed rider effect of a hunter carrying an eagle. Once, a wild eagle homed in on our solitary figures and wheeled over us, two times, before she blew down the wind.

We spent all day "hunting the eagle hunters," in Canat's phrase. Once, in a snowy pass, we struck a track: horses, a wolf, and fox, with blood in the fox's footprint! Canat was sure that we were somewhere behind our friends, but we could see nothing ahead but lava crests, a herd of grazing horses, and snow turning red in the lowering light. As the sun dropped behind us, turning the blue hills into dark sillouhettes, we admitted defeat and turned back toward the lights of Olgii.

We left early on the third day, and met the hunters on a pass just below and to the south of Manai's house. They had struck, and lost, a fox the day before, as Canat had guessed. We rode out in morning light.

I COULD NOT SEE THE FOX AT FIRST. THE EAGLE HIT THE WIND AS she topped the ridge but, instead of falling back, she cut into it and rose like a kite. Manai galloped forward at a speed that seemed reckless on the loose rocks, shouting. Now the fox appeared, fawn-colored and supple, cascading down the rocky steps like a furry waterfall. The eagle towered two hundred feet above, turned, and fell like a hammer. The fox dodged once, but somehow the eagle was now ahead of him, turning. The two arcs of movement converged in a cloud of dust, and all was still.

The fox was dead. It looked like a scrap of fur, a mere rag. Now that it had been killed, it seemed, physically at least, utterly insignificant. When I wheezed up to where it had fallen and turned on my camera, it whirred and rewound. I checked, and found no film in my pockets. I will swear that I smiled. I had been so intent on chasing and catching the quarry I had forgotten entirely about the mechanics of photography, which was exactly right and proper. Best of all, my last photo showed the eagle towering above Manai and the dinosaur back of the ridge, eternally poised over her prey. As in James Dickey's "The Heaven of Animals": "Their descent / upon

the bright backs of their prey / May take years, / In a sovereign float-
ing of joy."

And this: I felt liberated. Not to go home and write this, but to
relax and enjoy—the air, the cold, the company, the gold braid on
Manai's bag; sun on snow; the breath of the horses; Bayaan Olgii,
Mongolia; life; the ongoing hunt. I was, in that moment, certain in
a way I could not yet express that my eagle dreams had brought me
to where I wanted to be.

THE REST OF THE DAY, THE REST OF THE TRIP, WAS ODDLY LIKE
being at home, in the best sense of those words; not anticlimactic
but quotidian, full of small pleasures and comforts, the conversation
of friends, good meals. I had a double-vision sense that I was more
in my true place there than when actually at home in New Mexico.
Mongolia seemed, at least for the moment, more concerned with
daily and eternal things than the endless round of media, of persua-
sion, special pleading, political correctitude, and unnecessary rules
that took up more and more space in the US. People here bought
and sold, but weren't continually bombarded by messages to do so.
There was, at least so far, a blessed absence of soundtracks.

We had time for meals with Canat and Aika and the kids. We
shopped in the bazaar for mutton, little dried onions, and blocks of
green tea. Libby saw her first "sausages on the bone" there, curling
down in great loops from the ceiling of a shed, where whole sheep,
living and dead, were also displayed. Libby asked Aika what a peculiar, foot-wide, truncated cone of white fat was. She answered "camel
hump—fat for cooking." As Libby said later, it was strange to see the
inside of something you had been riding on.

The market also displayed two other central contrasts: Russian motorcycles with sidecars, and outdoor pool tables. If a bike's rider wore a helmet, he was a taxi driver. The pool tables exist in every market from Bokhara to Xinjiang to Olgii; I never did quite understand why. But it was a matter of my acceptance of such things as "normal" that I never thought to ask the question.

IN OLGII, CANAT WANTED US TO VISIT A SEER, A WOMAN HE called a "shaman," though she was also a Kazakh Moslem. I asked him, only slightly tongue in cheek, if the falcon-training imam at the mosque would approve. "But they are friends!" Religious lines in Central Asia are never as clean as westerners, or Saudis, would wish.

Kadycha was about thirty-five, and a relative of some sort of Aika's. When she was a child, out herding, she was struck by lightning. She had been "out of her mind" for a couple of weeks (he meant in a coma); when she awoke she found herself paralyzed from the waist down, but able to see visions and foretell the future. I asked the usually skeptical and "scientific" Canat what he thought of this. He smiled and shook his head. "I cannot explain. But she is right maybe ninety percent. Especially for biz-ness!"

Biz-ness indeed. Canat, ever the entrepreneur, was not just running custom tours. He was also opening a bar ("Canat's Bad Dog Beer Bar"—look for it when you get to Olgii!) but also looking to expand his export business. The silk road was open again for planes as well as camels, and we had packed more wall hangings into our duffel than I would have believed possible, even standing in it to pack in three more tightly rolled tapestries. Apparently Canat wanted Kadycha's imprimatur on our new mutual venture.

We went early, before ten, for once. Canat said the readings tired her, and that she was so in demand that she would be busy all day. She lived in a newly whitewashed winter house. Inside, her waiting room was bright, with wall hangings everywhere. The next room was, inexplicably, entirely filled with boxed TVs, VCRs, and electric components. She sat behind a low table, with her crippled legs and tiny feet curved under her. Her clothes were chic and her eyes as bright as a bird's as she chatted on a cell phone, rolling her eyes dramatically. She gestured to us as she seemed to first reassure, then admonish, then laugh, at her call-in client. Two young women waited on her. Although Canat would later tell us that all were Kazakh, she had a pale face and "Mediterranean" features, while her attendants both had copper-red faces and features more like an American Indian or even as Eskimo than any Mongolians I had yet seen. I wondered if, despite the Kazakh culture, whether shamans could still be of Tuvan blood.

She hung up and began to comically berate Canat. He actually looked embarrassed before he laughed—"Some jokes about me and Aika," he said later. Apparently her humor was notoriously bawdy. He encouraged us to ask three questions each; I asked the kinds of questions I always do: would my book sell? Should I, in today's climate, continue to write? Should I move to a city? Such mundane questions would hardly tax her, I thought, or cause her any embarrassment, as they were not ones likely to be proved wrong while we were in Olgii. She covered her eyes with her hands and quickly came up with yes, yes, and no; no surprises, although she did add through Canat that since I had never wanted to do anything but write it would be sad for me to give it up. Libby's questions were also pragmatic and straightforward.

Which left Canat to ask the hard ones: my health, Libby's, and warnings for our future business. She looked at me and told me I had bad lungs, but had recovered. That I once had constant heartburn (Canat: "hot, indigestion, acid"), but now took medication.

And that, last week, I had terrible pains in my right shoulder, but was now better. She then told Libby that she had "bad eyes": not hard, since she always wears glasses; and that she had seriously high blood pressure, which was under control with medicine, and that she *should* eat salt. For the record, all these were true, and Canat could have known only about my lungs. (The pains were an attack of pseudo-gout that I am still working out with my doctor; perhaps she should consult with Kadycha!)

On business, she gave us her blessing and told us to start right away, which pleased Canat, and that we should be aware of a fat American who, at this date, has not materialized. We paid her and emerged into dazzling sunshine to pass an already twenty-foot-long line of people waiting to see her.

SO OUT, AND ON: TO ULAAN BATAAR, MUSEUMS, SHOPPING, lunch at "Claire's," the familiar pleasures of a familiar town to which we were sure we would return. We packed our treasures: antique flint strikers, new art of Buddhist demons and camels; clothes from Surenkhor, some to keep and others to market; maps, scarves, an antique camel chess piece, a working flintlock rifle of recent manufacture and seventeenth-century design. Treasures of the orient, links to have in our old home when we missed our new one, or when the e-mail was down. At the airport, when we turned in our tugrugs, they were new, and no longer smelled of sheep fat. I had a bad moment when the customs inspectors pulled me out of the boarding line to the plane, fearing they wanted to confiscate my rifle. They just wanted to see what it was; when I produced a photo, they congratulated me on making such a fine purchase.

Epilogue

And *mon semblable, mon frère*, should I have gone? Should you? Yes, and maybe. Mongolia wants, welcomes—perhaps needs—us, and we may need them more than we realize. But do it right. Go with people who employ, enjoy, even *are*, local. Check your prejudices at the door. Americans in particular seem to have difficulty with (or fear) Moslems, and think they prefer Buddhists, perhaps because they mistakenly think that Buddhists have no rules. These tourists look to Mongolia as a bigger Tibet, only more accessible, with a soundtrack of Tuvan shamans throat-singing, no tractors, and a bunch of pet eagles that never kill anything. Be honest. If you feel like this, don't waste your money, or at least stick to tourist ger camps. The Kazakhs know better and have better things to do than pose for you.

Food and toilets are not issues to take lightly. When I had been back a month, a neo-Buddhist friend in New Mexico invited us over to show slides, offering a "vegetarian Mongolian dinner." I had to tease her. Mongolians, I said, barely know what vegetables *are*. One of the most sophisticated ones I met told me that they all "tasted like dirt" to him. They live largely on boiled sheep, hard cheese, tea, and vodka. But, she said, they're *Buddhists.* Yes, I said. If you fear what one Californian traveling in Zimbabwe called "dead food," stay home.

Toilets. There's nothing a seasoned backpacker can't endure. But, as one Peace Corps worker said to me, "All Mongolia is your toilet." And in areas with no trees, there's little privacy. The culturally strong Moslem *pudeur* and necessity to cover up can be particularly challenging in Olgii, especially with the mostly fat-and-meat diet, no real walled toilets, and sub-zero weather.

What all too much of the western world wanted, I could only see as a kind of romantic *picture,* a kind of colonialism where the Kazakhs of Kazakhland rode through a living museum of quaint Kazakh culture. Such travelers go to Ulaan Bataar (and, for that matter, New Mexico) talking about spirituality and complaining about the accommodations. In Ulaan Bataar, among the expatriates, I kept hearing that "they"—the Mongols, the Kazakhs—would have to "wake up to tourism," make better toilets, more reliable schedules, better accommodations, stop asking for overweight baggage charges even when the tourist is carrying a truckload of extra gear. For God's sake, *why?* Kent Madin seems to be doing very well by giving the braver tourists an authentic experience—there are no flush toilets in his tents!

Mongolia is changing. It has the internet and cellular phones; new fiber optic cables are being installed in Olgii even as I write. Ulaan Bataar is full of businessmen and Nongovernmental Organizations

(NGOs) doing well, and (sometimes) doing good. New citizens from Russia and the former East Germany abound. Tourists are ever more common, clutching their (*sometimes* accurate) *Lonely Planet Guide,* which my Mongol friends call, not without malice or at least irony, "That Blue Book." There are even Christian missions.

Mongolia is, at the same time, unchanging. The resurgence of Buddhism, or, rather, its reappearance, is astonishing; there are forty new temples, many in Ulaan Bataar. Pictures of the Dalai Lama are everywhere. There is a similar if smaller resurgence of Islam in Olgii; a Turkic brand, with a tolerance of saints and Sufism and even shamanism. The percentage of stock animals to humans is still the highest in the world, balanced by what remains one of the lowest population densities found anywhere.

Mongolia has problems; it always has. Anarchic Russia to the north, and the teeming and envious Chinese empire to the south, threaten its borders, and integrity; but then, they always have. There are problems as to what kind of economy will evolve; energy problems; ecological problems. Pressures to survive lead to too many domestic animals, which in turn threaten the range. And these problems have also been there for eons.

Perhaps because they have never had it easy, I believe they will survive: Mongol, Kazakh, Tsataan, Tuvan—all the nomadic people of the real big sky country. I look at the photo of Manai's lined face, smiling as he holds the hood, and I know I'll return "as long as eagles fly." If I must have a soundtrack, let it be of Kazakh horse music, with an order of sausage on the bone and a side dish of wild onions, mountains on the horizon, a rider sillouhetted on the near ridge, and a stone tomb in the foreground. I love Mongolia as it is and can be. Among other things that horrify our coddled society, it is still a free, wild country; where guns can still be allowed as carry-on luggage; where people smoke and drink and eat meat and ride horses and live to be eighty. They don't need our rules—yet. In a crowded world of increasingly enforced conformity, I hope I will always be able to return to a land of horses, mountains, endless skies, and eagle dreams.

"NOW ALL IS OVER I AM DELIGHTED THAT WE TOOK THE TRIP, as the sights we saw and the miseries we had to encounter will be something to think of as long as we live."

Colonel Peter Hawker, *Diary*
(7 August 1841)

$\mathcal{A}cknowledgments$

Rahmet! (Thanks!) to:

Richard Lowery, Eric Ratering, and Sasha Sorokin, for starting the ball rolling;

Clara Szklarz and Yuri Shelkaev;

My son, Jackson Frishman, for endless conversations, references and sometimes translations, and for the term "marmot paraphernalia";

David Edwards, Ed George, Jeremy Schmidt, and Matt Wells, and, above all, Kent Madin;

Editors: Sid Evans, Steve Jones, Diana Lutz, Terry McDonell, Cullen Murphy, and Amy Meeker;

Dan M. and "Patrick";

Greg Bowles, of the Peace Corps, and Rich Reading and Dr. Nick Fox, for biological information;

Larry Cary of Socorro, New Mexico, without whose computer expertise we would have despaired; Chad McCabe who came to our rescue more than once;

And above all to Acemgul, Akbek, Aralbai, Ariunbolor, Armanbek, Bolatbek, Sh. Canat, Aika, Kadan, Manai, Nyamdorj, Sailanhan, H. Siassi, the late R. Suleiman, Surenkhor, and the entire staff of the Bishrelt Hotel.

Tour Addresses

Kent Madin
Boojum Expeditions
14543 Kelly Canyon Rd.
Bozeman, MT 59715
Telephone: 800-287-0125
Fax: 406-585-3474
E-Mail: boojum@boojum.com
www.boojum.com

Canat Cheriyasdaa
PO Box 71
Bayaan Olgii
Bayaan Olgii Aimag
Mongolia
Local telephone: 04-3226
Fax: 071-208
E-mail: canat_c@yahoo.com

D. Bolatbek
PO Box 91
Bayaan Olgii
Bayaan Olgii Aimag
Mongolia
Ba-tours@chinggis.com

Bibliography

Andrews, Roy Chapman
Across Mongolian Plains
(New York, Appleton, 1921)

On the Trail of Ancient Man
(New York, Doubleday, 1926)
Indiana Jones hunts fossils. The second volume is better, but
harder to find. It is more about dinosaurs than ancient man.

Atkinson, Thomas Witlam
Oriental and Western Siberia
(Philadelphia, Bradley, 1859; reprinted by Asian Educational
Services, Delhi, 2000)

*Travels in the Regions of the Upper and Lower Amoor and the Russian
Acquisitions on the Confines of India and China*
(London, Blackett, 1860)
Priceless first-person narratives; much on "bearcootes."

Basilov, Vladimir (ed.)

Nomads of Eurasia

(LA Natural History Museum of Los Angeles County, 1989)

Scholarly and beautiful. Essential.

Becker, Jasper

The Lost Country

(London, Haddon & Stoughton, 1992)

Recent political history; much has changed since, though.

Berger, Patricia

Mongolia: The Legecy of Chingis Khan

(London, Thames and Hudson, 1995)

A lavish book on Mongol art.

Carruthers, Douglas

Unknown Mongolia (2 vol.)

(London, Hutchinson & Co., 1913; reprinted by Asian
Educational Services, Delhi, 1994)

Beyond the Caspian

(London, Oliver and Boyd, 1949)

One of the best, if you can find a copy.

Christian, David

*A History of Russia, Central Asia, and Mongolia: Vol. 1, Inner
Eurasia from Prehistory to the Mongol Empire*

(Oxford, Blackwell, 1998)

Cohen, David (ed.)

A Day in the Life of the Soviet Union

(New York, Collins Publishers, 1987)

A coffee table book with some good Kazakh and Mongol material.

Dementiev, G, *et al.*

Birds of the Soviet Union, Vol. 1

(Jerusalem, Israel Program for Scientific Translations, 1966)

One of the best regional ornithologies ever written. This volume, mostly on birds of prey, has much on falconry and local names.

Flint, Vladimir, *et al.*

Birds of the USSR

(New Jersey, Princeton University Press, 1984)

Still the best guide to the region. The newer Chinese oneis less accurate in ranges, and less detailed in natural history.

Hamilton Paterson, James

Playing with Water

(London, Macmillan, 1987)

Three Miles Down

(London, Jonathan Cape, 1998)

Not a thing on Mongolia, but serious references on photography and "media" in general, versus truth.

Hollinshed, Martin
Hunting with Golden Eagles
(Washington, Hancock House, 1995)

Kaplan, Robert
The Ends of the Earth
(New York, Random House, 1996)
One of the best contemporary books on Central Asia.

Lattimore, Eleanor Holgate
Turkestan Reunion
(New York, Kodansha, 1994 [1934])

Lattimore, Owen
The Desert Road to Turkestan
(New York, Kadansha, 1995 [1929])

High Tartary
(New York, Kodansha, 1994 [1930])
These Lattimore books are full of excellent information. *Desert Road* contains the most eagle material.

Legg, Stuart
The Barbarians of Asia: The People of the Steppes from 1600 BC
(This edition New York, Barnes & Noble, 1995; originally published as *The Heartland*, F S & G, 1970)

Levin, Ted
The Hundred Thousand Fools of God
(Indiana, Indiana University Press, 1996)
A wonderful book on Central Asian music, including some related to Kazakh. Contains a CD.

Lonely Planet Travel Survival Kit: Mongolia ("That Blue Book")
(Victoria, Australia, Lonely Planet, revised 1997)
Good on Mongolia; bad on Bayaan Olgii; flat wrong on eagles.

Man, John
Gobi: Tracking the Desert
(London, Weidenfeld & Nicholson, 1997)
One of my two favorite recent books. Excellent natural history.

Maraini, Fosco
Where Four Worlds Meet
(New York, Harcourt Brace & World, 1964)
Good on worldviews of Islam and Buddhism, among other
subjects.

Menzel, Peter
Material World
(San Francisco, Sierra Club, 1994)
A look at typical families' possessions, including a Mongolian
ger and other Central Asian material. Illuminating.

Mongolian Red Book
(Ulaan Bataar, 1997)
A useful starting point for Mongolian conservation, but be wary.
For instance, photos of the black or cinereous vulture are iden-
tified as two different species, like the falcons in the museum.

Novacek, Michael
Dinosaurs of the Flaming Cliffs
(New York, Anchor/Doubleday, 1996)
The other best recent book. R. C. Andrew's successor; better
science, less derring-do.

Polo, Marco
Travels
(London, Everyman's, 1983 [1908])

Psíhoyos, Louis
Hunting Dinosaurs
(New York, Random House, 1994)
Great Mongolian photos!

Reading, Richard
Dictionary of the Vertebrate Species of Mongolia
(Ulaan Bataar, 1994)

Stewart, Stanley
In the Empire of Genghis Khan
(London, HarperCollins, 2000)

Waters, Frank
Leon Gaspard
(Flagstaff, Northland, 1981)
The Taos artist, of Russian descent, traveled for years in
Central Asia.

Watson, Jeff
The Golden Eagle
(London, T & A D Poyser, 1997)
The last word on the subject, with fine illustrations, including a
Kirghiz eagler.

A Note on Conservation

A book could not be long enough to cover the issues of Mongolian conservation. Mongolia is lucky to have a great diversity of wildlife, from the conifer forests and lakes of the north, to the eroded dinosaur deserts of the south. Its population is small, and has had less of an impact than that of many other "Third World" countries. But its economy is precarious, and there are continuing pressures from outside.

It is certainly right to ban hunting of species like the snow leopard, the extremely rare Gobi bear, and the commercially vulnerable musk deer. But it would be best if Mongolia did not allow American and European pressure to make it fence off all its wildlife into theme parks where no interaction is allowed. If wildlife is seen as something that excludes people from their own habitat, the scene will be set for resentful poaching, as it once was in Africa. A better way might be to look toward such programs as CAMPFIRE in Zimbabwe, where rural residents can manage wildlife for ecotourism and hunting, and see direct benefits. I was pleased to see that eagle hunters are now licensed.

There is also an urgent need for money to do a real survey of what is at stake, a detailed blueprint of the nation's biodiversity. You can't save it if you don't know what is there. The *Mongolian Red Book* is a good start, but more of it is (admittedly) speculative than not. There is no reason that some of the fees paid by big game hunters could not go toward this, as well as directly to the local economy. Alan Parrott, or Hari Har Singh Khalsa, as he prefers, the American "Sikh" with the murky involvement in the falcon trade, has suggested that he manage the breeding and sale of falcons for the Mongolians, selling the birds to wealthy Arabs, with a built-in profit for himself. However self-serving, his falcon program might with proper modification fit into this scenario, though I'd prefer to see it managed by Mongolians. According to Tom Cade, world's authority on saker and Altai falcons, there are over twenty thousand nesting pairs of sakers in Asia. A preliminary survey of saker falcons in Mongolia has already been undertaken by David Ellis, Merlin Ellis, and Pu. Tsengeg; they found them abundant.

Britain's Dr. Nick Fox and Hunting Falcons International (see www.falcons.uk) are currently coordinating many conservation and research activities on birds of prey in Central Asia. Falcons suffer most from human ignorance. Populations in Kazakhstan dropped drastically when uninformed poor people attempted to catch all birds of prey, then found that no one was interested in buying babies, sick and injured birds, and species not used for falconry. In contrast, China has recently begun a legal trade in sakers to bring order, an end to poaching, and achieve a sustainable yield. The (American) Peregrine Fund is also starting to do research in Central Asia.

The International Snow Leopard Trust (www.snowleopard. org.islt) 4649 Sunnyside Ave N Suite 325, Seattle WA 98103, is now doing research on species other than the snow leopard, such as the rare Pallas's cat, also found in Mongolia.

All conservation must finally be local. As my Peace Corps informant wrote: "If only a few people benefit from tourism, there will be little incentive to comply with the laws." Mongolians and Kazakhs preserve the "memes" of some of our earliest interactions with animals. They, too, are worth preserving.

Berkut

(By Andrew Jackson Frishman, in the Anglo-Saxon manner. Jackson
wrote this poem at eighteen, and regards it as more of an exercise
than a success. But its premodern brio does give something of the
flavor of Kazakh life and song.)

See now! Day's dawning,
    Night's darkness despairing,
And fleeing in fright
    of the coming sun's fury
Whitening she withers,
    her dark veils withdrawing,
Fleeing away Westward,
    weary in waning.
At her back, pale and sallow
    now stabs her bright sister
Whose rays stain the clouds ruddy
    with garish Day's heraldry
And turn the pale snow-fields
    to satins ensanguined

With blood spilled not coldly,
    but in barbarous passion.

And as if to announce
    the morning's arrival
Three small earthly heralds
    come hastening from Eastward.
The first is a steed,
    short-legged and stocky,
But bred for hard riding,
    reared in rough weather,
Possessed in humility
    of that strange earthly pride
And lowly nobility
    found in the base-born
And to the lordly unattainable,
    though they claim they would loathe it
And yet desire this dearly
    that wealth cannot purchase.
So, too, is the rider,
    his face rough and reddened,
His eyes firm and focused,
    facing the West Wind.
Clad in soft leathers,
    cunningly crafted,
Humbly fashioned
    by hands weather-hardened,
He drives his steed downward,
    descending this mountain

In the land of his fathers,
    legends made living.
And standing on his strong fist,
    outstretched as in warning,

An emissary of Nightmare
    or else one of Heaven
Sits with wings furled,
    peering to Westward,
Sharp eyes seeking
    the slightest of movement.
An angel now fallen
    or friend with flight gifted,
Dagger-feet gripping
    the gloved hand that holds her;
Fiercer than goshawk,
    fleeter than falcon,
Imperial bird:
    the Kazakh berkut.

Were they now to view her,
    fell and proud-feathered,
Then wise men would swear
    that sweet milk and swallows' nests
Could not be too noble
    for so queenly a creature.
In cruel splendour wrought,
    each quill gleaming copper,
Bronze-feathered, brazen,
    She burns in the morning

With female fury;
    spawn of fell goddess
Yet by the gods bridled,
    dread wrath to be bearing
From Slavic Perun,
    who sends Heaven's fires,
Or Ukko and Akka,
    Ugrian sky gods,
Or Olympian Jove,
    lightning's liege,
His murderous vengeance
    with mortal fold meddling.

Any lesser a lineage
    would be far too lowly
For this most regal flier,
    and yet Fortune's fancy
A place on Earth has ordained her,
    among Earth's creatures dwelling.
And Man, in his own way
    than the gods no less noble,
Has wooed their fell daughter
    with wearisome waiting
Three days and three nights
    in tireless vigil.
The gods' golden princess,
    In grandeur, though hooded,
Sits through the night sleepless,
    on swinging perch balancing

So that rest be not found
    and fear thus be banished
By hunger and weariness,
    for welcome food waiting
And finally accepting
    when anger's forgotten;
For thus in the taking
    of food trust will flower.

When comes the cold winter
    in frozen silks white-clad,
Summer's warmth fading
    her fair bounty failing,
Forsaking the sheep-folds,
    they fare to the fields
And small sheltered canyons,
    game to be seeking.
They hunt deer for food,
    wolf and fox for soft fur-pelts.

There are some who live sweetly,
    sheltered in cities,
In peace and prosperity,
    their needs all provided,
Who turn a blind eye
    to cold, brutal Nature
And her would deny,
    deeming that death
Were unnecessary
    to nourish the living.

Such kind would condemn
    these proud Kazakh hunters,
Accusing of cruelty
    the falconer's killing,
Forgetting in folly
    the forces of Nature
Which throughout the long ages
    drove to evolve
Berkut the brazen-winged,
    of birds the most mighty,
Forged in that foundry
    where Darwin's smiths fashion
Forms more fantastic,
    for life suited more fully,
Cherishing wheat
    while scorning the chaff.
And Nature's selection,
    through long aeons laboring
Has cast from the crucibles
    of Killing and Famine
This bird, bred for hunting,
    not blind to the need
For deeds grim and dreadful,
    gore-stained and deadly.
When eagle was wrought
    the gods wrought a weapon
Which is itself a smith
    in the forge of selection;
A Kindly One, killing
    in ruthless compassion,

Better breasts breeding,
 dross to be smelting,
For thousands of centuries,
 cruel Nature's culling.
For what maid would make
 A mother more cruel
Than Nature, whose rearing
 Is nascence and death,
Who grants us our lives
 Yet gives us such justice
Offspring or extinction
 as our chromosomes merit?
To then try and cheat her,
 headstrong and hopeless,
Would seem highest folly
 And yet we succeed
In usurping her laws;
 We strike pacts with strangers
In common purpose,
 pursuit of our prey.
And pardon is granted
 to young that would perish
If Man in his insolence
 ingenuity lacked.
So what thing be nobler
 than to unite against Nature,
Overcome enmity,
 ancient grievance forsaking,
And hunt with strange comrades,
 hawks, horses, and hounds?

And now aloft high in Heaven,
    she soars on her huge wings,
The wild wind bridling,
    wheeling and climbing
Upon Death's steed riding,
    dread of the Earth-bound,
She folds her vast pinions
    and toward her prey plummets,
Striking in silence,
    deadly and swift.
And the man as he watches,
    earnestly waiting,
Is now fully certain
    that in such a silent
And brooding dark Heaven
    Thunder was born.

Index

A

Acemgul, 170, 171, 173
Across Mongolian Plains (Andrews), 51
Airag (drink), 161, 162
Aitmatov, Kirghiz Chingiz, 16
Akbek, 166, 171
Altai mountains, 1, 102–3
America, eaglers in, 31–32
Ames Free Library, 13–14, 51
Andrews, Roy Chapman, 4, 15, 51, 84
Animals
    Kazakhs' attitude toward, 137
    life among, 16–17, 203
    minds of, 18–19, 21
Apachito, Paul Jones, 86
Aquila (eagle), 17, 18, 19
Aralbai, 132–42, 155, 177
    eagle of, 134, 138–39, 141–42
Ariunbat, 85–87, 155–56
Ariunbolor, 156
Armanbek, 133
Artemisinin (drug), 58
Atkinson, Thomas Witlam, 50, 134

B

Bakker, Bob, 84, 85
Bakyt, 115, 118, 119
Baldach (crutch), 13, 122
Bayaan Nuur, 107–8
Bayaan Olgii, 1, 6, 43, 91, 93–99
    bazaar in, 94–95
    landscape around, 101–5
Baz Nama Y Nasiri, 36
Beagle, Peter, 70
Beebe, William, 14
Beijing, 61–63
Berkut (poem), 205–12
Beyond the Caspian (Carruthers), 12, 14

Bibliography, 195–200
Birds. *See also specific species*
    in Beijing, 63
    and dinosaurs, 83–85
    in Mongolia, 104, 127, 127n, 131, 137
    of prey, and conservation, 202–3
    training in Central Asia, 48–53
    in Ulaan Bataar, 79–80
Bishrelt Hotel, 68, 73–75
Bodio, Libby, 46, 59, 153, 183
    with Bolatbek, 173, 175
    in Bozeman, 45, 47
    on Kazakh livestock, 103–4
    with Manai, 2, 179
    notes of, 180
    and seer, 185–86
    and Stephen's illnesses, 56, 57, 167, 170
Bodio, Stephen J.
    at Aralbai's, 132–42
    with Bolatbek and family, 171–77
    and bulbuls, 131–32
    with Canat's family, 107–11, 129–30
    eagle of, 22–24
    flight to Mongolia, 59–63, 65–67
    in/around Bayaan Olgii, 88–91, 93–99,
        103–5, 142–44, 148–49, 183–84
    influences on, 9–17, 51
    with Jambitai, 106–7
    and Kazakhstan film, 36–43
    love for birds, 3–4
    malaria/pneumonia of, 56–58, 167–70
    with Manai, 1–3, 144–48, 178–83
    in Natural History Museum, 82–85
    with Nyamdorj, 159–65
    proposals for story, 45–48
    at Sailanhan's, 125–29
    and seer, 185–86
    at Suleiman's, 111–24

in Ulaan Bataar, 67–82, 85–87,
    155–59, 186
  in Zimbabwe, 53–56
Bolatbek, D., 165–67, 169–70
  home of, 170–71
  tour address, 193
  trip to family, 171–77
Bozeman (Montana), 45
Brighton Beach Station, 37
Buddhism, in Mongolia, 189
Bulbuls, 103, 131–32

C
Cade, Tom, 72
CAMPFIRE (Communal Areas Management
  Programme for Indigenous Resources),
  54–55, 202
Carnie, Kent, 22
Carruthers, Douglas, 12, 14, 28, 96, 103n,
    180n
  on bulbuls, 131
Central Asia. *See also specific countries*
  birds of prey in, 202
  history of bird training in, 48–53
  landscape of, 66–67
  and Native Americans, 86
Cheriyasdaa, Aika, 100, 148, 183
  and Stephen's pneumonia, 165–70
Cheriyasdaa, Canat, 2, 67, 69, 86, 91–94
  apartment of, 97–98, 166–67
  businesses of, 72–73, 153, 177–78, 184
  and clothes, 95, 96, 97
  in Disco Bar, 98–99, 143–44
  family of, 100, 125, 129–30, 144–45
  and F.I.R.E., 155
  on Lenin's works, 95
  on monuments, 102–3, 131, 180
  and seer, 184–86
  tour address, 193
  trip with Nyamdorj, 158–65
China, 2
Chingiz Khan, 4, 15
Chloroquine, 57, 58
Choibalsan, 5
Chor, 127
Choughs, 79, 128
Cummins, John, 24n

D
Darwin, Charles, 14
Deel (clothes), 76
The Desert Road to Turkestan
  (Lattimore), 53
Dho gazza (netting), 38
Dickey, James, 182–83
Dinocheirus, 84–85
Dinosaurs
  and birds, 83–85
  in Mongolia, 4
Disco Bar, 98–99, 143
Domboro (guitar), 139, 147
Dorchester (Massachusetts), 10

E
Eagle owl, 123
Eagles, 17–19, 21–22, 120–21
  Aralbai's, 134–35, 138–39
  Bodio's, 22–24
  and falconry, 24–25, 28–32, 34–36
  and Kazakhs, 12–13, 114n, 138
  Kazakhstan film of, 38–43
  Khairatkhan's, 175–76
  Lattimore on, 52
  Manai's, 1–3, 145–47, 180
  passage, 127, 146, 180
  quarry of, 3, 14, 20–21, 146, 182
  Remmler's, 27
  Sailanhan's, 125, 126–27
  Suleiman's, 112, 113–15, 119–24
  training, 29–30, 121–22, 146–47
Easton (Massachusetts), library of, 13–14
Edwards, David, 44, 60, 67
Central Asian/Native American project, 86, 87
  on courtesy, 70
  and F.I.R.E., 155
  on Kazakhs, 68–69
  photo essay of, 47
Ellis, David, 202
Ellis, Merlin, 202

F
Falciparum. See Malaria
Falconry, 17, 22, 24, 24n
  Atkinson's account, 50–51
  and eagles, 17, 24–25, 28–32, 34–36,
    38–43, 114n, 121–22
  Marco Polo's description, 48–50
  Remmler on, 27
Falcons. *See also Falconry*
  endangerment of, 71–72
  in Mongolia, 131, 202–3
  sakers, 83, 127, 127n, 202
Fansidar, 58
F.I.R.E. (Flagstaff International Relief Effort),
  155, 163, 165
Flaming Cliffs, 4
Fleming, Peter, 15
Fossils, in Mongolia, 4, 83–85
Fox, Nick, 202
Foxes, and eagles, 3, 14, 51, 121, 126–27, 182
Francis, Chris, 111
Freya (eagle), 33
Frishman, Andrew Jackson, 48, 59, 101, 153
  poem by, 205–12
Frishman, Harry, 153

G
Gandanlegchinlen Monastery, 78–79
Gaspard, Leon, 13
George, Ed, 59, 60, 105, 112, 117, 129
  and bulbul, 132
  photographing Aralbai, 140–41
Gers (tents), 6, 77, 86
  Jambitai's, 107
  Nyamdorj's, 161

Glenn, Warner, 99
Gobi bear, 201
Gobi Desert, 4, 66
Golden eagle, 17–19, 120
    and other raptors, 35–36
    picture of, 11–12
Gorbatov, Vadim, 49, 50
The Goshawk (White), 130
Grave mounds, 102–3, 103n, 180, 180n
Grizelda (eagle), 35
Gyr, 127, 127n

H
Hares, 52, 117n
Harting, J. E., 50
Hawker, Peter, 190
"Hawk Roosting" (Hughes), 22
Hazara (restaurant), 69–71
"The Heaven of Animals," 182–83
Hess, Karl, 53, 58
High Tartary (Lattimore), 12, 52
The Hound and the Hawk (Cummins), 24n
Hughes, Ted, 22
Humphrey, William, 25
Hunting
    with birds, 48–53
    controlling, 201–2
    foxes, 121
    Kazakhstan film of, 39–43
    wolves, 146
Hunting Falcons International, 202
Huntington, Betsy, 148

I
Ichinnoron, Mora, 88, 89
International Association for Medical
    Assistance to Travelers, 56
International Snow Leopard Trust, 203
Islam
    and animals, 16
    in Mongolia, 189

J
Jambitai, 106–7
Jungle Book (Kipling), 9–10

K
Kadan, 2, 145, 147, 181
Kadycha, 184, 185
Kazakhs, 4, 43–44, 50, 52, 68–69, 189
    attitude toward animals, 137
    and butchering, 161–62
    and eagles, 13, 114n, 127, 138
    houses of, 107, 170
    physical diversity of, 166
    and Stalin, 43, 131
Kazakhstan, 2
    eagle project film, 38–43
    Russian bases in, 131, 160
Kaztour, 165
Kepesh, 146, 179
Khairatkhan, 175–76

Kim (Kipling), 15
Kipling, Rudyard, 9, 15, 165
Kirghiz, 44, 50
Krakel, 32
Kublai Khan, 48–50
Kurghans (graves), 102–3, 103n, 180, 180n

L
La Capitale-Doula, 158
Lariam (mefloquine), 57, 58
Lattimore, Owen, 12, 28, 51–53, 96
Levchine Alexis de, 14
The Lion King, 18
Loft, John, 36
Lorenz, Konrad, 29
Lowery, Richard, 30, 31

M
Madin, Kent, 45, 46, 47, 81, 148, 153, 188
    tour address, 193
Malaria, 56–58
Manai, 144–48, 177, 178–83
    on eagles, 146–47
    home of, 145
    hunt with, 1–3, 182–83
Mansell, Floyd, 99
Maraini, Fosco, 16
McCarthy, Joseph, 52
McDonell, Terry, 46, 59
McGuane, Thomas, 133
Men's Journal, 59
Migjid Janreisig Süm, 78
Mongolia, 4–7, 187–90
    advice for visitors, 187–88
    birds of, 104, 127, 127n, 131, 137
    business buildings in, 81
    conservation in, 201–3
    elevation of, 5
    fossils in, 4, 83–85
    government of, 5
    people of, 4
    religions in, 188
    Russian bases in, 160
    size of, 4–5
    tour addresses, 193
Mongolian Red Book, 202
Mongols. *See also Mongolia,* 4, 43, 189
    festival of Tsagaan Sar, 148
    jewelry of, 86
Montgomery, Monty, 152
Mundy, Talbot, 15
Murphy, Cullen, 153
Musk deer, 201

N
Native Americans
    and Central Asians, 86
    and eagles, 32
Natural History Museum (Ulaan Bataar),
    82–85
Navajos, 86
New Mexico, 16, 96–97

Nomads, 5, 189
 in pictures, 12–13
Nomads of Eurasia, 12
North American Falconer's Association, 34
Nyamdorj, 159–65

O
Oriental and Western Siberia: A Narrative of
 Seven Years' Explorations and Adventures
 in Siberia, Mongolia, the Kirghiz Steppes,
 Chinese Tartary, and Part of Central Asia
 (Atkinson), 50–51, 134
Oviraptor, 84

P
Parrott, Alan, 202
Paterson, James Hamilton, 150, 151
"Patrick," 32–34, 44
Peacock, Doug, 104
Peregrine Fund (American), 203
Peregrines, 17, 71–72, 127
Peterson, Roger Tory, 17
Pigeons, 79–80
Polo, Marco, 48–50
Primaquine, 58
Protoceratops, 84

Q
Quinine, 57

R
Raptors, training, 29
Ratering, Eric, 30
Ravens, 79
Red Desert (Wyoming), 19–21
The Red Queen (Ridley), 102
Reminisces (Remmler), 25
Remmler, Frederick W., 24, 25–28, 32, 33–34
Richardson, H. H., 13–14
Ridley, Matt, 102
Romans, and eagles, 17, 18
Rungius, Karl, 179
Russell, Charles M., 130
Russia
 bases in Mongolia/Kazakhstan, 160
 falconry in, 30–31, 34–35

S
Sailanhan, 125–29
Sakers, 83, 127, 127n, 202
Salmon, Dutch, 99
Schell, Orville, 53
Schneebaum, Tobias, 130
Sebright, Sir John, 24
Shipman, Pat, 103
Siassi, 91–93, 103, 128, 135–36
Siberia, 2
Snow leopard, 201, 203
Sorokin, Sasha, 30
Soviet Union. *See Russia*
Spanish culture, and animals, 16
Stalin, Joseph, 43, 131

Steppe eagle, 23
Suleiman, R., 111–24, 177
 eagles of, 112, 113, 114–15, 119–24
 house of, 111–12, 113–14
 hunting with, 116–19
Surenkhor, 159, 163
Szklarz, Clara, 12, 37–38, 40–43

T
Tarbosaurus, 85
Tarr, Bryant, 178
Tavanbogd Uul, 5
Tawny eagle, 23
Theropod dinosaurs, 84
Tours, 193
Tsagaan Sar, 148
Tsataan, 189
Tsengeg, Pu., 202
Tugrugs (currency), 7, 81
Turkestan Reunion (Lattimore), 53
Tuvan, 189
Tyrannosaurus, 84, 85
Tyson, Ian, 130

U
Ulaan Bataar, 5, 6, 65, 67–68, 75–82, 165, 186
 airport, 88–90
 birds of, 79–80
 changes in, 155–59
 hotel in, 68, 73–75
 Natural History Museum, 82–85
 restaurants in, 69–71, 158–59
 temples in, 78–79
Ulaan Huus, 173
Unknown Mongolia (Carruthers), 103n, 180n
Uzbeks, 43

V
The Variation of Plants and Animals under
 Domestication (Darwin), 14
Vigne, Gace de la, 24n
Vizzo, Claire, 158, 186
Vultures, and eagle, 127, 127n

W
Walker, Alan, 103
Wells, Matt, 47, 59
Where the Spirits Dwell (Schneebaum), 130
White, T. H., 22, 130
The Wisdom of the Bones (Shipman and
 Walker), 102–3
Wolf, Tom, 55
Wolves, and eagles, 14, 146
World Monitor, 12

Y
Yuri, 37–38, 40–43
Yurt, 6, 77

Z
Zimbabwe, 53–56
 conservation in, 54, 202